MW01165482

WHEN THE TULIPS BLOOM

BY

SUSAN E. MILLER, MS, RN

COPYRIGHT © 1993 by Susan E. Miller

All rights reserved. No part of this book may be reproduced in any form or by any means, graphic, electronic, or mechanical, including photocopying, or any information storage or retrieval system, for sale, without written permission from the author, except for brief quotations included in a review.

Edited by Jerena Burdge-Rezvan

Cover Design by Thomas Taylor of Thomcatt Graphics in cooperation with
Melissa Miller

Vista Publishing, Inc.
473 Broadway
Long Branch, N.J. 07740
(908) 229-6500

This publication is designed to provide educational information with regard to the subject matter covered. It is not a technical nor clinical reference book. All readers are encouraged to seek medical advice and diagnosis by a qualified physician. This book is sold with the understanding of the buyer that if medical advise or other expert assistance is required, the services of a competent professional should be sought.

Printed and bound in the United States of America.

ISBN: 1-880254-08-5
Library of Congress Catalog Card Number: 93-60937
First Edition

U.S.A. Price $12.95
Canada Price $16.95

DEDICATION

To Liz:

Without YOU, this book would never have been written! Thank you for everything my special friend!

A loving and heartfelt thanks to Glenn, Melissa, and Mom who loved me even when I was unlovable.

Thanks to a very special family: Shawn and Will - you were there every time I needed you. I love you both.

Van and Vere: thank you for all that you did during those first few hours of Glenn's illness. I love you both.

Dear Suzanne - thank you for being the best sister to Glenn. You were exactly what he needed. Larry - thank you for letting your wife stay with us when we needed her.

To my friend Nancey Sabo for the books, long distance phone calls, and your support of my decision when I wondered if I'd done the right thing.

A very special thanks to Nolan and Terry, my pastors, who prayed with me in times of complete despair. Thanks to my church family and my Sunday school class who prayed for me when I couldn't. To Nancy, Diane, Mona, Kim and all my friends at who helped me and cared for me when I couldn't think straight.

Dr. Ongkiko whose surgical expertise and knowledge gave Glenn and me our lives back.

To Dr. Malcomb: Thank you for listening to me, for being there, and for caring enough to answer even a strangers question. You are a true professional who cares about all of his patients. Thank you for giving me a chance for tomorrow.

To Susan and Barb: you two are the best nursing role models around. You two could write a book about how to care for, understand, and love cancer patients.

To Dr. Kurtzman: Thank you so very much for putting me back together. You gave me hope in the face of terror. You showed me that I could be whole again and my life and my body image would not be excised along with the cancer. Thank you for Boobette, for understanding, and caring about me and my feelings.

Dear Debbie: What can I say to you except that because of YOU I am where I am today. Without you I know I could not have come so far. You gave me courage to realize that it was my body and my choice as to what would happen to me. You heard desperation in the voice of a stranger and gave me a choice that changed my life. You are truly a great nursing model.

I could go on and on thanking all people who helped me. Words cannot express how I really feel, but I thank the Lord everyday for all of you. You make the world a better place because you give a part of yourselves everyday to those you meet.

I LOVE YOU ALL!

Thank You,
Susan

MEET THE AUTHOR

SUSAN E. MILLER, MS, RN

Susan Miller has over twenty two years of nursing experience in the areas of critical care, recovery room, oncology, nursing research, and nursing education. She earned her diploma from the Good Samaritan School of Nursing in 1969. She received her Bachelor of Science in Nursing in 1982 from Miami University (Ohio) and her Masters of Science in Nursing in 1985 from Ohio State University. Susan has contributed to articles concerning nursing research and has lectured extensively on various professional and health related topics.

As a nurse educator and clinical instructor, Susan has taught in Diploma and Associate Degree programs. In addition, she has served as a Visiting Instructor at Miami University (Ohio). She has developed and presented numerous hospital and community based education programs.

Currently a Clinical Nurse Specialist in Critical Care at St. Elizabeth Medical Center in Dayton, Ohio, Susan is actively involved in the development of competency based programs for nurses, research, and direct patient care. She volunteers many hours as a resource and advocate for women who have been diagnosed with breast cancer.

Susan resides in Middletown, Ohio with her husband, Glenn and daughter, Melissa. As a family, they enjoy skiing and participate in a wide variety of activities within their church.

CHAPTER ONE

Living A Real Life Nightmare

I sat looking at the strange hospital room. I was cold and I pulled a blanket up over my shoulder. The cold air from the ugly old register blew directly on me, and as I gazed around the room, it was dreary. I looked over at the bed where my wonderful husband lay. His color was ashen gray and his respirations were shallow and labored at times. My mind was jumbled. How could this happen? I didn't understand. How can life change so quickly, in just a matter of a few moments?

I had known Glenn since high school. He was the smart, red-headed kid who would run by my bus and wave at me. I went to our Valentine's Sweetheart dance with him, but he kept stepping on my toes. The girls all thought he was a hunk because he ran track, but to me he was just the red-headed guy who looked like Mr. Murley, my English teacher.

After we went to the Sweetheart dance, he started calling me regularly. My grandmother was staying at our house because my sister, Shawn, had pneumonia and my Mom was a nervous wreck. Grandma would always say, "It's that Miller boy again."

We went to a couple of basketball games, but one of my old boyfriends asked me to the Senior Prom. I would rather have gone with Glenn, but he made me mad, I don't remember why now, and I told Nick I would go with him. I heard Glenn had asked a girl from another school.

I went to the French Shop to buy my formal. My Mom and I had such a great time picking it out. It had a plain yellow bodice and tiny yellow flowers on the long fitted skirt. They told me I would be the only one with this formal.

When Prom night arrived, I could not wait to see the girl Glenn was bringing from another school. I kept looking at the door, waiting for him to arrive. I felt beautiful, my hair flipped just right, and I didn't have one broken nail. Nick and I had been friends since grade school and we always had a good time together.

When Glenn came in the door, my heart literally stopped. He looked so handsome in his tuxedo and the girl on his arm was a knockout, with a formal exactly like mine!

I didn't even talk to Glenn again until we were on our Senior Trip to Washington, D.C. We went to a little Italian restaurant and he bought me my first spaghetti and meatball dinner. My Dad never liked restaurant food so we seldom ate out. We had a nice time but I didn't see him again before he left for the Air Force Academy that June.

I dated a lot of different guys that summer, but I kept thinking about Glenn. He had never held my hand, let alone kiss me, but yet he constantly invaded my dreams.

I left home the Fall of 1965 to go to Good Samaritan School of Nursing. I had wanted to be a nurse my entire life. My Mom said I was three years old when I said, "I be nurse when I get big." Well, that time was finally here.

The dorm seemed dark and dreary. We didn't have real beds, instead they were big orange plastic chairs that folded out into chair beds. My roommate was Judy, but we didn't seem to have much in common. She was loud, and besides that, she smoked. She didn't study till after lights were out, usually under the covers with a flashlight.

It rained all Fall. I was homesick and all the boys I had dated during the summer had gone away to college. The girls all had steady boyfriends, except for a few girls who had never had a date. Judy talked me into sending Glenn a letter. I had clipped his picture from the newspaper which had announced his appointment to the Academy. So I sent him a letter -- just a newsy letter, and signed it, "Your friend, Susie."

I hated chemistry. I had gotten B's in high school, but it was different here. It was a college course taught by one of the professors from one of the local colleges. All those formulas! I caught my long hair on fire with the Bunsen burner in Chemistry lab, and my Anatomy lab partner dropped a scalpel on my foot and I had to go to the emergency room. I was so homesick I would cry every time I heard my Mom's voice. "How bad do you want to be a nurse?" I would ask myself daily. My friend Diane and I studied hard, but we struggled with Anatomy & Physiology and Chemistry.

Midterms were awful. I had never taken tests that hard. I had studied all the wrong things. I knew my name would be on the "black list" for those on probation. On the way to see if my name was on the list, I stopped at the mailbox and found a letter from Glenn. His, too, was just a newsy letter, until the end when he told me he was serious about a girl named Amy. By the time I had finished reading the letter, I was in the hallway where the dreaded list was to be posted.

I didn't want to look, but yet was compelled by some inner force, hoping against hope. The list was longer than I had expected, but there was my name right in the middle. Oh no, what would I tell my parents, my friends? I was a failure, a flunky.

I ran down the hall and as I rounded the corner I met Sister Dorthea. She was so kind. She looked at me and told me it was not over yet, but I just ran across the street to the dorm. I didn't care it was raining.

I went home that weekend and my Mom and I made a plan. I got tutors for Anatomy and Chemistry. I studied like I had never studied before. When finals rolled around before Christmas, I was ready. I didn't leave a single blank on any test. The "black list" that was posted did not have my name. I had gotten an A in Chemistry and a B in Anatomy & Physiology. I had asked an old friend to our school Christmas dance and things were getting better for this student nurse. I hardly ever thought of Glenn Miller anymore.

Then one March day I got an invitation in my mailbox. It looked like maybe one of my old friends was getting married, but when I opened it I realized it was an invitation to an Air Force Academy Ball at Wright Patterson Air Force Base. I was to be the guest of Cadet Glenn O. Miller. WOW! Were the girls in the dorm impressed! But how would I get there? I had no idea where Dayton, Ohio, was. I had never even driven to Columbus by myself.

When I showed my Mom the invitation, she was excited for me. Together we wondered how I would get there. Then she looked at the date. It was her and my Dad's wedding anniversary. She would convince dad to take her to Dayton. Remember this is the man who only ate hamburgers out.

Yes, Yes! We convinced Dad to go to Dayton. We didn't have money for a formal and I was hard to fit, a size 3. I wasn't about to wear my formal from the Senior Prom. The one from my Junior was short and it just didn't seem appropriate for a Military Ball.

My cousin Linda had a beautiful formal for her prom. It was beige and orange. How many formals were those colors. No one would have one like that. Mom and I took in seams and hemmed and made it fit me, but so it could be let out again in case Linda needed it. Long gloves were all too big for me and white ones just didn't go. We searched and searched and finally we found a little short pair of beige gloves with little bows on the back of the hands. We dyed an old pair of shoes orange and away I went to Dayton.

My Dad found a motel and nice restaurant close to the base. He even hired a taxi to take me to the Officer's Club where I would meet Glenn. The taxi driver took me to a side door where a uniformed officer ushered me into a room full of girls all dressed in the most gorgeous formals I had ever seen. A lot of them knew each other and were talking about the "cute cadets." I didn't even know if I would remember what Glenn looked like. It had been almost a year since I had seen him.

A lady came to tell us about the receiving line and how to greet all the officers and wives of those who were sponsoring the dance. At the end of the receiving line was the General, but at the beginning was his wife with several officers and wives in between. We were to greet and shake hands with each one. The General's wife took one look at me and she gasped but said, "Where did you find those gloves? My daughter Susan and I looked for beige gloves all over Dayton." I looked behind her and there stood a tall beautiful blond in my formal, but with long white gloves. I guess I wasn't to ever go anywhere without someone having a dress like mine.

At the end of the line I met Susan's father, the General, who mumbled something about being glad I could come, then saw Glenn come from the shadows to take my arm. We danced and danced. I met all his friends from the Academy. We took a long walk by all the English Tudor homes and we talked about our dreams for the future. When he kissed me with the blue runway lights in the distance, I knew my life would never be the same. I knew I loved this handsome blue-eyed cadet and, yes, I knew he loved me too.

Tears began to run down my face as I thought about how much I loved him. How I remembered so distinctly almost 20 years before at that Air Force Academy ball looking at his face, knowing that I would spend the rest of my life with him. Now he lay there on the brink of death and I thought, "We're too young. He's only 42. How can he die so young? Oh God, please don't let him die."

I thought back to the events of the day before. What a busy time it had been. Both of us were working hard. He worked for the government, a GS-14, and I was a nursing educator at a large hospital. We both were running seminars that day and we talked about what a busy schedule we had. I had two seminars back-to-back, one during the day and one in the evening. He had a seminar during the day and then a party in the evening. But, we agreed to meet for dinner at the Marriott since my seminar was there. Bernie Segal, a man known for his help books for people who are sick or dying of cancer, was the speaker and I was helping to coordinate the seminar with my department from the hospital.

About 3:00 I called Glenn's secretary and left a message for him to call me back. Eventually Glenn called and we agreed to meet about 5:00. At 5:00 things were kind of quiet, but there were other seminars going on, so the hallways were full. I kept glancing at the door looking for Glenn. Suddenly I saw him walking across the parking lot and thought how handsome he looked in his new suit. I realized I loved him more than I had 20 years ago. I reminded myself how lucky I was to have such a good marriage.

I tried to get to the door as quickly as I could, but it seemed that people were just coming from everywhere. When we saw each other there wasn't a need for words. We just grasped hands and walked quickly, exchanging a few greetings on the way to the dining room. I chatted about the Bernie Segal seminar and all the things I had learned about how to achieve acceptance of things that happen to you in life, how to accept illness, and how it would help me with my wellness education. He talked about his seminar, the things that had gone well, the problems, and the party later that evening.

As we waited to be seated, we were holding hands and the look on our faces must have told the waitress that we needed a quiet place away from the rest of the crowd. She seated us underneath an old antique picture at a little table just for two. We sat holding

4

hands, exchanging even more information about the seminars we had attended during the day and the hour passed very quickly.

When it was time to return and help with registrations, I began to walk him to the door. He told me he would be going to the party and anticipated being home around 10:00 p.m.. We kissed quickly and he headed out into a very brisk, cool, October night. I watched him walk across the parking area and went quickly back into the motel.

About 8:00 I asked my manager, Pat, if I could leave then, a bit early, as I was tired and would be running another seminar the next morning. Pat and I had a great relationship. She was flexible, but always aware of what was going on in her department. As soon as she said, "Sure, go ahead Sue." I grabbed my coat opened the door , and was shocked by how cold it was. There was a cold, damp rain coming down and I thought now I'm going to have to wash my hose when I get home. Running across the parking lot, water splashed up and ran down the back of my legs. The leaves were blowing eerily across the road.

I drove home thinking about all the things I had to do before I could go to bed. There was a dinner at church tomorrow night and I had agreed to make a broccoli casserole, so I had laid out the things before I left that morning. I got home, changed clothes quickly, and began to make the casserole, being almost finished when Glenn came in the door. We laughed about his timing, agreeing he was now off the hook.

We quickly finished up the dishes, put them in the dishwasher, and went upstairs to go to bed. It was close to 10:00 p.m. and continued to talk about the seminar the following day. As I had to be at work by 6:00 a.m., we set the alarm clock for about 4:30 a.m. Glenn commented as he got into bed on how very tired he was, but kissed me quickly and we snuggled up. I went to sleep almost immediately as I, too, was very tired.

Suddenly I awakened as I felt Glenn jerk. He was lying on his left side, on the edge of the bed, and as I turned to see what was wrong, he just rolled right out of bed. I heard an awful cracking and realized it was his head hitting the night stand. I screamed his name repeatedly asking if he was OK. But he was face down on the floor with his body wedged between the bed and the night stand.

I screamed, and I picked him up with a strength I didn't know I had, moving him over on his back. When I saw his face I couldn't believe he wasn't breathing and was blue. I thought automatically A-B-C, CPR, but my mind didn't want to work. I heard this crazy voice, and realized it was mine, saying, Lord, Oh God, please help me. Don't let him die.

It was at that point I heard my cohorts' voices at work. We all teach CPR and ACLS together and I heard them say to me that as I had witnessed the arrest, thump him on the chest. CPR. Two quick breaths then fifteen compressions. I observed no breathing. Check the pulse. No pulse. He's dead. I'm going to be just like my mother; I'm going to be a widow. And the tears came.

5

But suddenly I found myself doing CPR, thinking, it was a witnessed arrest, I need to thump him on the chest. I took my fist and I hit him as hard as I could across the sternum. His body jerked, and I felt for a pulse. As I couldn't really feel anything, so I continued to do two quick breaths and restarted the compressions. When I went back to do two more quick breaths, I looked at his neck and I was thrilled to see pulsations. It was very rapid, but definitely a pulse. So I gave him two more quick breaths, and I ran for the phone.

I dialed 911, but the phone wouldn't work, making a crazy whirring sound. I dialed again and the same thing happened. I realized I didn't have the time to keep playing with the phone. So I pushed '0' for the operator and thankfully she came on. I gave her my name and address and requested an ambulance immediately as my husband had coded. She told me to hang on the phone. Don't hang up.

I continued to breathe for Glenn for a couple of seconds. Suddenly I saw his body stiffen. He became what we call 'decerebrate' (a stiffening of the body with hands turned inward). I watched as he began to jerk in one arm, then the other, then his legs. He clenched his teeth, his tongue was between his teeth and blood squirted everywhere. I realized now he was having a seizure and asked myself what do I do? He opened his eyes and I noticed his pupils were completely dilated. His color was ashen and I was afraid he might bite his tongue off. Somehow, with a strength deep down inside of me, I managed to pry his mouth open and push his tongue back in his mouth. I realized I didn't have anything to put in his mouth but couldn't think. He began to seizure more and more violently. The jerking was the worst I had ever seen as a professional.

The operator was still on the phone telling me that they were sending me help. I was screaming and crying for help I did realize, at that point, how hysterical my voice sounded. I began to yell out the window, but I don't remember opening it. I kept yelling for someone to help me.

The seizure continued as I glanced at the clock. I knew it was just a little bit after 12:30 a.m. and we hadn't been in bed very long. I estimated it had probably been happening for about five minutes though it felt much longer..

I continued to breathe for him because there were no respirations and his color was so poor. He wasn't hard to breath, it was easy to get the air in. I just breathed into his mouth and his chest would rise just like in CPR.

The operator kept talking to me and I would yell out the window. She told me help should be coming and it seemed like hours. In my coherent mind, I knew that it was only minutes, but it seemed like an eternity. I heard the sirens as they came around the corner and I could see the red lights as they reflected on the window.

I continued to breathe for him but then, suddenly, Glenn stood up. I thought irrationally he's going to be OK as he reached out as if to take me into his arms. But when

6

I looked up into his face and all I saw was dilated pupils, I realized he wasn't with me in consciousness. He fell on top of me, again seizing violently, harder then before. I was wedged between his body and the floor, my head was turned and I felt it beating between the floor and the metal bed frame.

As I heard the sirens come closer, I thought how upset he would be if he had hurt me. But I couldn't get myself loose. He was too heavy, and I didn't have any more strength. He continued to seize violently. His color remained poor and I realized he needed more oxygen. So I reached up, put my mouth on his, and breathed into him, using every ounce of breath and strength I had. At that point he became flaccid and I was able to get out from underneath him. But again his body was face down on the floor. I picked him up and rolled him on to his back again and began to breathe into his mouth.

By that time the sirens were louder and I knew that they were on the cul-de-sac. As I heard them come into the driveway, I yelled out the window for help. When they asked me to open the door I told them to break it down.

I breathed again two more breaths and looked down at my red, sheer, low-cut nightgown. Knowing the paramedics would be in my bedroom, I stood up and found my robe at the end of the bed. I quickly put it on as they hit the door the first time. It only took two big thrusts and the door burst open.

They were up the stairs in a flash, and as they came towards me, I gave Glenn two more breaths. They asked me what happened but I told them I didn't know. He had just rolled out of bed in full blown arrest. At the same time they were putting on their latex gloves, I felt an unexplained anger that they were taking so much time putting on gloves and getting forms together. I said, "Why? He doesn't have AIDS. I'll breathe for him."

At that point they said, "Ma'am, we'll take over now."

I turned and I saw my neighbor, John, a doctor. He was there reaching his hands out to help me, urging me to get dressed repeatedly when I insisted I could go to the hospital in night clothes. He put his hands on my shoulder and he walked me into our large, walk-in closet an order to get dressed, and he gave me a hug.

I realized that the paramedics were talking to me, asking about age and weight. I looked and it seemed that they were just standing there, doing nothing. I told them to just get him in the ambulance and take him to the hospital. I assured them I'd answer later. I just wanted them to take him to the hospital. I knew I wasn't making sense, and again John reassured me it would be OK, he gave me another hug and I shut the door to the closet. I grabbed a pair of jeans, an old sweatshirt, put on my tennis shoes, and came out.

By that time they had Glenn on the stretcher and oxygen going. He was trying to sit up and didn't seem coherent at all.

John told me he had a seizure and was postictal.

I looked at him and reminded him I had been here when he had the seizure. I felt frustrated and frightened as I watched them carefully take him down the stairs. It was hard to watch them cart him down the stairs, as he would try to sit up almost at every step. He was confused, did not understand what was going on, or what had happened. After I helped them put him in the back of the ambulance, one of the paramedics took me by the arm, opened the door to the ambulance and told me to get in.

Tears were running down my face as I looked back at our new home. We had only been there a few months. It was our dream home and we had spent the last year designing and having it built. We were so proud of it but I suddenly realized my priorities were all in the wrong places. Houses didn't mean anything, but the people in your life have meaning. My love and concern for my husband was all that mattered at that moment.

I turned back and could see the side of Glenn's face as the paramedics surrounded him. I watched them hold the IV up and heard them describe to him what they were doing, that he had a seizure and was in an ambulance. I heard him moan for the first time, turned around and reassured him I was there and wouldn't leave. It sounded as if he responded and I thought at least knows who I am. I asked the paramedic if he knew it was me and Glenn answered in a very slurred voice, but I could understand, yes, his response. The tears continued to stream down my cheeks and I realized I was getting my sweat shirt wet.

It was then I became aware of the ambulance driver. He turned around and got within an inch of my face. With dirty blonde hair and foul-smelling breath, he began to yell at me that everything was going to be OK. He ordered me to stop crying. But I couldn't. I reassured him I wasn't hysterical and had every right to have tears. But again he continued to yell at me.

Suddenly a policeman appeared at the window of the ambulance and told me they would try to make rounds on the street frequently as the front door was damaged. I realized I couldn't leave the front door the way it was since no one else would be home. Our daughter, Melissa, had just left a few weeks before for college. My mind cleared a bit and I suggested he use the alarm system upstairs on the bedside table. He could push alarm delay, and prop the door shut so that it looked as if it were locked. I watched him walk up the sidewalk and into our house.

It seemed like there were lots of people, fireman, policeman there to help me and I could see the policeman through the upstairs curtain turn the light off, come downstairs, and watched him prop the door shut. It looked like the way the house always looked at night.

Again I turned around to check on Glenn, but I couldn't see anything but the backs of the paramedics. I asked them to check on how Glenn was doing and if he were awake and then began to think. With my medical background I knew that this was not going to be good. There were just a few things it could be: a stroke; a heart attack; or some type of aneurysm or brain tumor. I even hoped that since he had been to a party that evening maybe someone had put some drugs in his drink. He had only had some 7-Up, but you never know. People could have put something in his drink.

As I asked the paramedic again how he was doing, he stepped out of range and I could see Glenn's face, with the oxygen. With very slurred speech he told me himself that he was OK and I just thanked the Lord that Glenn knew me and could respond. He raised his hand, waved to me, and I was pleased he could at least move one hand.

We backed out of the driveway and I turned around just to watch where we were going as we drove down the familiar streets on the short trip to the hospital. I heard the paramedics talking on the radio, telling the hospital they were coming. The man with the dirty, greasy, blonde hair once again said very loudly to me that everything was going to be OK and I just wanted to slap him. Had I been hysterically crying and screaming, I would have understood it. But he was mean and so cold.

I looked at my hands folded in my lap, and thought about what I should do next. All at once we were at the hospital, the paramedic was at my elbow, and I was ushered into one door and they took Glenn through another. I found myself in the middle of the waiting room. There was my sister, Shawn, who had been working upstairs, and Will, her husband waiting for me. I just collapsed into her arms and she hugged me while I cried. Somehow I had remembered to get a purse and to make sure I had the insurance card, amazing myself that my own brain cells were functioning. They motioned for me to sit at the desk, asked me the routine questions, and I gave them the card. I heard them talking about the man they brought in as a code and remembered how many times I'd heard that, never dreaming that some day it would be my husband they were talking about.

The double doors opened and I got a glimpse of Glenn's face in the light. I was appalled to see his eyes were as black as coal, with big lumps in front of each ear that were bluish-black, like black ping-pong balls sitting on his cheeks. He had bruises all over his face, neck, and shoulders to the nipple line. I thought how strange that they stopped at the nipple line and resume again in the groin area, going all the way to his feet It amazed me how clinical the mind can be, even in a crisis involving a loved one.

When they finally let me go back with him I grabbed his hand and asked if he knew me, thrilled with the response that he did, even using my nickname, Missy. I asked him to squeeze my hand with each of his, to wiggle his toes, and he could move everything. I praised the Lord, knowing Glenn was aware of who I was and could move all his extremities. When he complained about being unable to open his eye and the pain, I realized he must have cut his eye as he rolled out of bed hitting his head on the nightside table. It looked terrible, swollen and bloody.

The doctor and the nurses were giving him Dilantin IV and ordering a Foley catheter. He was placed on the monitor. As I watched the monitor, I saw normal sinus rhythm, no abnormal beats. It didn't seem he had a heart attack. In my clinical mind I knew that it could only be those two or three things that had happened to Glenn. My mind didn't want to think about that and I just turned away.

My sister was there and I remember her just putting her arm around me, trying to provide comfort. I felt such a warmth and compassion from this little sister, suddenly all grown up and here I was leaning on her. At that moment I realized that I needed to talk to Nolan, our pastor, and I needed to call Glenn's brothers, Van and Vere. Will handed me some quarters. Going to the pay phone right outside the waiting room, Will helped me with the numbers while I dialed and told everyone what happened. I knew my mind and my body were still working, but I felt like I was functioning in another world as I finished.

I hit the electrical door opener and returned to the cubicle holding Glenn. I still couldn't believe what had happened. Why couldn't I have seen this tragedy coming? As a nurse, I get paid to assess patients and yet had not seen what was happening to my very own husband. But the logical side of my mind knew that you can't always see what you are so close to.

When the doctor came in to check him again, Glenn moaned and reminded him about the eye pain. His tongue was swollen and his mouth was still bloody. As the nurses came in it seemed as if they looked at me with sad eyes, and some of them had tears in their eyes. I realized everybody knew how serious this situation was. I watched them clean his tongue and his mouth but he continuously complained about his eye, and would squint. Glenn knew everybody, he could move all extremities and I felt a ray of encouragement and hope. I continued prayed silently for the Lord, to please let everything turn out OK.

I don't know how long we sat there but Shawn finally had to go back to her patients, and Will stayed a while longer, but had to go back to work. Van and Vere came, their faces were pale and frightened, but they were so supportive. I couldn't remember from one moment to the next, I felt so tired, exhausted and confused. Nolan, our pastor, came and had prayer. He couldn't stay for very long, he had a big day planned at church the next day. It was 2:30 am by then.

When the nurses came to transfer him upstairs, I wanted to take him to the Intensive Care Unit, but the doctor said he would instead be taken to a step-down unit. As of that time he was awake, wasn't seizing, and there was no reason to send him to the ICU. It didn't really matter to me as I was going to stay with him and not leave him alone.

Once transferred to a room, I kept looking at Glenn but I knew I had dozed off for awhile. Suddenly I awoke to an odd scraping noise, the curtain had pulled apart and this crazy eyed little old man peers over at Glenn. I looked at his face and could see that he was confused, and he didn't know what is going on. He ripped the curtain shut again.

Glenn aroused at the noise and I told him about the patient in the next bed, a little old man, who was confused. That went on for an hour or so: every few minutes he would rip open the curtain, and close it again, rip open the curtain and close it again.

One of the nurses came in, very young, blonde, blue-eyed and supportive. She asked me if there was anything I needed as I watched her take Glenn's vital signs. It just seemed so unreal to see this happening to him but she did let us know they planned to transfer Glenn to another room so we could get some rest.

At this point I couldn't believe it was 6:00 a.m. in the morning and I felt as if I were caught in a time warp. As the head nurse came in the door, I recognized her right away. We had worked together in the past and it was so good to see Joyce, her warm friendly face, and her comforting smile. She knew how to take charge and we moved him quickly, bed and all, to the other room. Glenn never opened his eyes, he just laid and gritted his teeth. He looked strange and pirate-like, with a patch on his eye, and the swollen tongue that made his mouth seem full. Once he was settled I sat down and it seemed a little warmer in that room, with another plastic chair. As I started to lay back to see if I could get some rest, Joyce came in and suggested that I go home for a little while, take a shower and come back. She assured me he was resting, with good vital signs and Glenn agreed, telling me to go home.

I thought about the fact that I didn't have any car and no way to get home. Then I remembered that Van and Vere were out in the waiting room and Shawn said she would stay till I got back. I was glad to get home, even for a short time.

I don't know who had taken care of the bedroom. When I walked up the stairs, everything was clean, the bed made. There was no sign of the events that had happened the night before, except in my mind. As I looked at that floor, my mind vividly remembered him lying there with the dilated pupils, and the tears flowed again, my voice wailing in anguish. The cry that came out of me seemed to be that of a wild animal. I cried and cried as I laid at the foot of the bed, but realized I was wasting precious time, and needed to get up, shower, clean up, and be back at the hospital. It was daylight, and chilly now. I knew that I would have to dress warmer than I had dressed the day before, so I hurriedly took a shower, combed my hair and even stopped to put my make-up on, because I knew Glenn would want me to do that.

Vere took me back to the hospital and I talked to my sister Shawn, who told me they had taken Glenn to be CAT scanned and he commented on their need to check out his head. I couldn't believe how clear his thought processes were, he knew everything that was going on. I thought it couldn't be something wrong with his head, he was able to think so clearly after everything he had been through. I sat down on the chair and noticed that my legs were having muscle tremors and knew how really tired I was. I laid my head back and the next thing I knew I had drifted off into a very deep sleep. I guess I had relaxed a little bit, thinking that something was being done, and I would have some answers very soon.

A short time later they brought Glenn a breakfast. It was clear liquid, but it was a breakfast. He sat up and attempted to drink a little bit, but admitted his tongue hurt too badly. He couldn't really swallow very well either. The IVs were still going, and he couldn't remember he wasn't to get out of bed. He kept trying to get out of bed and go to the bathroom. Every little bit, we would remind him he didn't have to go the bathroom with a tube in your bladder, it's taking care of that. But in just a few minutes, he would sit up again and try to get out of bed. Pretty soon we put the TV on, for some noise factor.

I tried to answer his questions as he asked me what really happened. He kept complaining that his chest hurt and I finally told him of having to hit him on the chest when I couldn't find a pulse. Suddenly through the door came Dr. Kresge, the kindest, gentlest, most wonderful physician I had ever known. Dr. Kresge was just a few years older than Glenn and I. Nine years before, he had been diagnosed with leukemia and wasn't expected to live, but yet he had beat the odds and stood there at the foot of our bed, looking healthful and young. With a very serious look on his face, he looked at us and said, "Glenn and Sue, I have some good news and I have some bad news. Which do you want first?"

I shot a sideward glance at Glenn and said, "Give me the bad news first," with Glenn shaking his head in affirmation.

Dr. Kresge looked at us and said, "I'm sorry to tell you this, but Glenn you have a brain tumor."

CHAPTER TWO

A Life Flashes By In My Mind

I just sat there. My mind didn't want to focus, but just to run around in my head. All kinds of things began to run through my mind. I remembered our wedding day and how our minister had pronounced us Mr. and Mrs. Glenn Campbell. I remembered my Dad walking me down the isle and telling me he loved me. I looked at the wedding band on my hand and remembered what our wedding invitations had written on them:

> *As these rings are linked together around the cross, it is*
> *our prayer that our lives will be eternally bound together*
> *by love and that our Lord Jesus Christ will be the head of*
> *our home and the center of our lives.*

Glenn and I had saved our money and honeymooned in Hawaii for ten days. When we finally made our destination, the Air Force Station in El Segundo, California, we were ready to set up our first home. Our things arrived on a rainy Friday and I was so excited I couldn't wait to start making our apartment look like a real home. I unpacked lots of boxes and lifted and carried, helping Glenn.

I had not had a period since Glenn and I had been married twelve weeks before, but that afternoon I started having cramps. I'd never had cramps before and they were very bad. Glenn took me to the base hospital and they just told me to go home with a hot water bottle. I began bleeding very heavily and started passing lots of clots. I called a friend and got the name of her doctor. When I called, I could not get an appointment until Monday. By Monday most of the heavy bleeding had stopped, but I was sore from all the cramping and nausea. The doctor told me that I was probably miscarrying. After he examined me, he determined that I was about eight weeks pregnant. The pregnancy was most likely twins, but I had lost one. I was however, definitely still pregnant. Our daughter Melissa was born November 15, 1970.

She was the most beautiful baby I'd ever seen, our pride and joy. She was a happy baby and never gave us any trouble. She was even sleeping through the night by her second night home. We took her everywhere with us. My doctor suggested that we wait a while to have another baby as I had a hard labor that lasted twenty-eight hours.

I decided to go back to work and took a job in the CCU at one of the large hospitals in California. I would be working the 3-11 shift. My first night back to work, I had a kidney stone and wound up missing three days of work. This was my second kidney stone and I hoped my last.

I liked working in California. They were so progressive medically and the patients who had brain surgery woke up faster, were brighter, and less impaired that the patients I'd seen back home. Patients with brain tumors and craniotomies always scared me. I went to special classes and seminars trying to learn as much as I could, but the fear never totally left me.

When Melissa was almost a year old Glenn was reassigned back to Dayton, Ohio. It was a great assignment, only three hours away from both our families. I got another job in a large hospital working as nurse in both ICU and CCU. Again, I worked the 3-11 shift so that Melissa could have at least one parent home most of the day. Glenn and I adapted to this schedule and it worked for us for many years. We bought our first house with a GI Loan and things were going well except for those crazy kidney stones that dropped like unexpected time bombs whenever they felt like it.

When Melissa went to first grade, I found myself lonely and wanting to do something different. I decided to go back to school for my Bachelors Degree in Nursing. Glenn and I had also become involved with our local church. Glenn was a very good actor and had a tremendous ability to memorize, so when the choir director needed someone to memorize an extra long part for the Easter Cantata, Glenn was chosen. He did an excellent job and our parents came to see him in his debut. I played a minor part and Melissa played one of the children in a scene. That Easter morning Melissa went forward to be baptized and we were now all members of the church.

We decided on the Fourth of July to go to Kings Island Amusement Park. On the way we stopped in a place called Middletown to look at some new homes that were being built. By the end of the week we were the proud owners of a new home. Our house sold for top price, we had three bids all offering more money than we were asking. We felt the Lord had truly blessed this venture of ours.

Melissa grew-up in the new house. When she was in Junior High School, I decided to back and get my Masters Degree in Nursing. I only applied to one school and that was Ohio State. I had just finished a year of teaching in the Associate Degree program at Miami (Ohio) University. I enjoyed the teaching, but felt that I needed more education. I continued to work part time in ICU and CCU. I prayed to God and that if He wanted me to do this, I would be accepted into the program and then I would know that this was His will. My friend Ruth and I were number nine and ten selected for the incoming class. So, off to Grad school I went.

Those were fun years but very demanding. I am such a perfectionist and was bound and determined to beat Glenn's Cum in his Masters program of 3.8. Two and a half years later I graduated with a 3.9. I took a totally different job than I had ever had before as a Nursing Education Coordinator. Glenn, Melissa and I remained active in our church.

By this time, Glenn was out of active Air Force duty but continued to work for them as a civilian. Things were going well. Melissa was a teen-ager and I was still plagued with kidney stones. It seemed every time I would mention having another child, I'd have another kidney stone instead, so we just gave up on the idea. After all, we felt we had done an excellent job the first time! Melissa was beautiful, a model teenager, never giving us a moments grief.

As Melissa got older and with Glenn and I both working days, the bathroom situation became a real chore in the mornings. I would sit on the floor to put my make up on because the bathroom was so small only one person at a time could get in. We decided to knock down a wall to enlarge the bathroom but when we looked at the cost it was terrible. The alternative was to buy a lot in an area across from where we were living and to build our dream house. After all, we weren't getting any younger and felt it was now or never.

We spent the whole year designing our new home. We went to home shows and open houses to be sure that we would get the most for our money. We moved in March of 1989. All the horror stories we'd heard about other couples building their homes didn't happen to us. Everything went smoothly except for a delay in the sale of our older home.

Melissa graduated from High School that spring. She did not graduate at the top or at the bottom, but somewhere in the upper half. She did well in things she liked and was looking forward to going away to school. She chose a small Christian College in Northern Ohio, Defiance College. I felt it was too far away from home but I was outnumbered and outvoted. We spent most of the summer getting her ready. Roommates, friends and classes consumed our discussions.

All too soon the end of August came, and Melissa was gone. I missed her terribly and cried a lot. Glenn missed her too, but not to the same extent that I did. Glenn and I went on a couples retreat at church. The retreat was held on the site of the band camp Melissa had attended and made me sadder than ever. I made Glenn take me home. By the end of the first month I began to adjust, and Glenn and I were having fun doing things together. It was a wonderful time learning to be "just the two of us...."

But now those words were haunting me as my mind once again brought me back to reality. A brain tumor?

CHAPTER THREE

The Wait

How in the world could this be happening? I asked Dr. Kresge what was the good news? Since he had just told us Glenn had a brain tumor, how could there be any good news?

He said, "The good news is that it does look at this point like it's in an operable place. I'm going to call in a specialist, a Dr. Ongkiko. I'm going to have him look at the Cat scan and have him write it up. He'll be in this afternoon to see you."

I sat there questioning if he really was the best. I knew that he had done good work there, but still wanted to be sure he was the best we can get. I didn't say anything to Glenn, but I had to find out who was the best.

The nurse came in to give Glenn his bath and he was giving her a hard time, he didn't want to let go of his pajama bottoms. He was holding on for dear life. I assured her I would give him the bath, explaining I was a nurse as well as his wife. I gave him the bath like I had for hundreds of patients before him, thinking he might resist at first, but he didn't. He also allowed me to clean his still sore, swollen tongue. When I got down to his feet, I remembered that he had had surgery on his big toes for ingrown toenails, and found the dressings were bloody and needed to be changed. I asked the nurse to get me some dressings and together we bandaged his toes, all the while I thinking I was bandaging his toes, and he has a brain tumor. My mind just raced, I was numb. I realized I had better make some phone calls. I was the only one who had the news of the diagnosis.

How do you tell someone's parents that their son has a brain tumor? I remembered vaguely wanting so desperately to talk to my mother the night before and telling the lady on the phone, I wanted to talk to my Mom. I went out to the phone and with some quarters that Will had previously given me, I started telling people the news.

It was pretty early yet, but I went ahead. I called my Mom and talked to her. I called Glenn's Mom, I didn't know how to tell her, other than the truth, and I just blurted it out. I didn't really think about how ill she was herself. I tried to be as sensitive as I could, but the diagnosis was so devastating. I told her that if she felt up to all they had better come. Even though she told me she was too weak and couldn't come, I felt Glenn needed to see her and she needed to be there if even briefly.

I also realized that I had better call Glenn's office, dialed them and I talked to one of the ladies in the office, Jerry. I told her I needed to speak with his boss, Merlin, and explained how serious the situation was. Merlin came on the line, I could hear in his voice but he didn't quite understand what I was trying to tell him. When he offered to help me however he could, I asked him put Glenn on medical leave, because he has a brain tumor. I could hear the silence on the other end of the phone as if he didn't have words to say. I remembered I had called my boss in the middle of the night and told her husband to let her know I wouldn't be at work, so I called my cohort, Nancy. She told me not to worry about anything, she would take care of everything for me. She offered to come down in a little while with my calendar to work things out. How grateful I felt and I remember thinking I would never forget Nancy and Merlin for the kindness and support they gave me. At least I didn't have to worry about our jobs. Glenn had over four months of leave, so I knew we would be OK financially for a while.

I knew I had to call our daughter at school. I got through and found the strength to tell her. I didn't want her to drive home and sent Van to go get her. I could tell by the sound of her voice she was annoyed that I wasn't going to allow her to drive home, but I was afraid she might be too upset and have an accident. I couldn't handle the prospect of anything else happening to our family.

It wasn't very long after that when my Mom and Shawn came to sit with me. The day sort of dragged on and people from the church came in and out. Nurses that I knew in the hospital came, nurses I didn't even know, to give their support. They started taking care of me, too, telling me to go eat, get some rest. But I couldn't eat, my tongue didn't work; it didn't push food down anymore. I wasn't hungry, and couldn't really sleep though I felt tired. I just paced.

Our friends, Bruce and Liz were on vacation. Bruce is an Emergency Room doctor. I felt I wanted them there badly, needing to talk to Bruce as he could help me understand some of this. Should I try to find another specialist? Joyce, the head nurse, came down and when she asked if I was OK. I asked her to help me decide what to do. Should I have Glenn sent either to St. Elizabeth, where I work, or down to University Hospital in Cincinnati? I didn't think I wanted him to have a craniotomy in such a small hospital. I wanted him to go somewhere where they did lots of craniotomies. Though she assured me Dr. Orgkiko was good, I remained unsure. I didn't doubt his abilities, but wanted Glenn to get the best care, with the most modern equipment. I didn't know what to do but decided I did want to talk to Dr. Kresge about it, quietly. Joyce led me to her office to make the call.

When I called Dr. Kresge's office, the line was busy. He had such a busy medical practice, I needed to dial and re-dial. I sat there and looked at the pictures of Joyce's grandchildren on the wall, of her family and thought will Glenn ever even get to see Melissa graduate from college or see his grandchildren? Finally I got through and told the receptionist I needed to talk to Dr. Kresge, that it was very important. I explained to her what had happened and she, too, was supportive.

Dr. Kresge and I spoke for some time, and he told me that he would recommend Dr. Ongkiko to anyone, he was an excellent physician. But he also told me if I really felt I wanted to take him somewhere else, to go ahead and he would help with whatever the decision would be. I asked him what would you do and he responded by saying he couldn't tell me what I should do.

When I hung up the phone, I began to cry. I still didn't know what to do. I talked to some of the nurses as I came out of the office and they said the same thing, I would have to make that one on my own. In confusion I returned to Glenn's room and heard him talking to someone, thinking I would have to curb those visitors because he didn't need to be talking that much. I entered the room and there stood Dr. Ongkiko.

Glenn had his good eye open and introduced Dr. Ongkiko, adding he would do the surgery. He would get rid of that brain tumor. Dr. Ongkiko turned around and recognized me. Thoughts began running through my head, that the decision had already been made. Glenn wanted Dr. Ongkiko, but I wanted him to go somewhere else, or did I? I didn't want to make Dr. Ongkiko angry. I watched him go through his neuro exam and I remembered that he was a very good doctor. His accent was heavy and sometimes I could understand him and sometimes I couldn't. When I asked him to repeat things, he was very patient and explained everything to me.

He told us he thought it was a benign tumor. I found that hard to believe with the family history Glenn had, a mother with cancer, uncles with cancer, and two aunts who had died of the disease. How can that be? I wanted to scream with joy even though it didn't reconcile with the facts.

After he left, Glenn commented he really liked Dr. Ongkiko and they had a good rapport. I still questioned if we needed to go to a bigger medical center, but the more I thought about it, the more I realized that it was more important that Glenn feel confident with his doctor. If he liked him, I would go along with it.

Nolan returned as Glenn was taken to have an EEG. He walked with me down the hall and we stood outside the EEG room and talked. We could see them doing the EEG through the little glass window, and we prayed. I asked him if he would please have prayer time for Glenn tonight, and he assured me that they would.

I turned around and walked back to Glenn's room with the nurse finding my Mom and Shawn there. They were trying to feed me again, but I kept refusing.

Van had left early in the morning to pick up Melissa, but they were late returning and I was getting nervous. Melissa had taken the news very well and didn't seem to be out of control. I thought of what a strong young woman she was and how proud I was. She had a few tears in her eyes, but she said emphatically she thought it was going to be OK. Since they thought that it was benign, they would just take it out, and her Dad would be fine. I could see she had a strength that came from within as she gave me a hug.

It seemed like different people were coming and going. I went down the hall and tried to make a few more phone calls to tell people. My friend and co-worker Nancy appeared out of the elevator, and said she had lost my calendar, but had written down the things that I had been working on. We took a few moments to write out my schedule and worked out how to manage work responsibilities. All I could say was thank you for the relief and freedom from my job she gave me in that way.

As I walked back into Glenn's room, I realized that Merlin and Al from his office were leaving. They had been to see Glenn while Nancy and I had worked on my schedule. Their faces were white, and they were visibly shaken. I thought they were going to pass out in the hall. They looked at me and said they shouldn't have come, they didn't know he was so sick, he looked terrible. The words just seemed to fall hurriedly out of their mouths. They gave me a hug and encouraged me that they would take care of everything at work. Merlin would take care of Glenn's sick pay and make sure he got paid. I thanked them and told them how much I appreciated their help.

The evening seemed to pass quickly with friends coming in and out. I tried to decide whether to go home or stay for the night. My sister said she would watch him part of the night, if I would agree to go home for a couple of hours and try to sleep. We agreed at 2:00 a.m. I would go home, but as the evening wore on, Glenn became more and more disoriented and confused. He couldn't remember to stay in bed, he kept trying to get out. Finally I told the nurses to put a bed alarm on his bed as I was afraid he would fall out and hit his head. He didn't need a head injury on top of everything else.. At 2:00 a.m. my sister came to relieve me and the nurses put the bed alarm on. Every time he would raise his bottom up off the bed, it would trigger the alarm.

I went home but didn't sleep. Instead I walked the house alone. I didn't know what to do. I finally lay down and fell into a rather frenzied sleep for a couple of hours. Vere had said he would take me to the hospital around 6:00 a.m. but I felt as if I was in another world. I looked out the window and two or three inches of snow covered the ground. It was eerie seeing the snow on those funny Halloween lanterns and pumpkins.

As I went downstairs a chill flowed through my body. I wanted to sit down and let the tears come, but I decided not to cry, but instead to put this in the Lord's hands. I got down on my knees and tried to pray, but no thoughts or words would come. Yet I knew the Lord understood what my mind could not express at this time.

The doorbell rang and it was Vere. As I stood up I noticed that the mail had been piled on the hall table. I just pushed it aside and went out the door. On the way we saw a house that had a whole row of pumpkins lining the entire sidewalk and were covered with snow, which gave the entire yard a strange orange glow. The leaves on the trees had funneled the snow as it fell, causing the branches to break or fall to the ground. I had never seen anything like it in my entire life. Everywhere we looked, we saw this strange combination of Christmas and Halloween.

19

When I returned to Glenn the nurse was taking his vital signs. He looked more like himself, a little less swollen. Shawn was sitting with him, but she looked tired. She told me he had had a restless night and I gave her a big hug and sent her home. I watched her walk down the hall thinking of my love for her and my sincere appreciation for her help.

As I turned around, Glenn was frowning at me. and heartily expressing his disapproval of those bells on his bed. I almost chuckled as it was the first thing that I had thought about that even seemed remotely funny. He didn't want to be wired; he wanted to get out of bed. I tried to explain to him and admitted I had been responsible for the alarm. We turned it off while I was there. Every time I turned my back, though, I would see him trying to slide out the end of the bed.

Melissa came in and I went down the hall to get myself some coffee. When I came back, she told me he had tried to get out of bed, but looked at her and went "Shhhhh", as if not to tell that he tried it again. We had to keep putting him back in bed since he couldn't remember he was not supposed to get out of it. The child-like behavior seemed a bit funny.

Glenn's parents and sister live in Zanesville, Ohio about three hours away. When I called them with the news about Glenn's tumor, they were in a state of shock. My in-laws are the best in-laws a person could have. Glenn's Mom had just been diagnosed with cardiomyopathy less than a year before and I worried about her heart. Glenn's sister, Suzanne, was just a few years younger than Glenn and they had a wonderful caring relationship.

When Glenn's sister and Mom arrived it was amazing how he perked up and seemed more alert and oriented. His mother came in a wheelchair and Melissa pushed her in. She appeared so frail as I watched her reach for his hand as tears ran down her face. I saw the look of motherly love as she reached for Glenn's hand, and she wished it were her.

Glenn's Dad, the silent type, stood beside the wheelchair observing all of this. He came over and lightly gave me a hug across the shoulders. Only a couple of times in the last twenty years had my father-in-law ever came up and hugged me. The first time was when my father died.

Surprisingly enough the day passed quickly. The nurses came and went, and I stayed in my plastic chair, sleeping a bit. Friends and neighbors came and my dear friend and neighbor, Bobbie, arrived and offered help in any way. Glenn's sister, Suzanne, also a nurse, was supportive. Her husband, Larry, just stood and looked sad, but I could tell he was worried by the look on his face. Larry was generally jovial, always joking, but this time he was quiet and distant. Interestingly though, Glenn talked very coherently to them and made jokes. They decided to go and get him some things to listen to. Glenn is an avid reader and his sister returned with humor tapes from the library for him to play, along with a tape recorder. It was amazing to see how they were rallying together, trying to provide support and keep him occupied.

We put the TV on, found some humorous things, and told a few jokes that made Glenn laugh. People from our church came and everybody commented on his positive and humorous attitude. In the afternoon I had to go to the bank, check on the house payment, and make sure his check had deposited in the bank. Suzanne stayed with Glenn while I did these errands.

I spoke with Dottie, one of the tellers at the bank. She could tell I had been crying and when she asked what was wrong, I told her my sad story. She helped me make some plans, just in case things didn't go right. She told me about her husband's recent crisis: He had been struck by lightning, and survived, but it changed his whole life. He divorced her and was trying now to do everything he had ever wanted to do.

On the way back from the bank, I began to reflect about that day. I had missed seeing Dr. Ongkiko as I had been home cleaning up. They had told me he would be in later that evening to give us a full report and a game plan for what the future was going to hold for us. As I drove back to the hospital, I was once again plagued by those incessant tears that just didn't seem to want to stop. When I got back to the hospital the whole family was there and Shawn had brought me something to eat. Though I felt very supported, the pain in my heart just didn't go away. Glenn had written letters to his brothers and had started letters to all of his family telling them what to do if he didn't make it. I just felt sick inside.

Dr. Ongkiko walked in, and we got a good laugh as he went to turn the light on above Glenn's bed and grabbed a get well balloon instead. He began to poke and prod and to assess Glenn's mental status. Shawn, Suzanne and I stood there as he told us he wanted to get a better look at Glenn's tumor, and wanted to send Glenn to Christ Hospital for a Magnetic Resonance Imaging (MRI) to get a picture of what the tumor looked like, I asked if he would have to go by ambulance since our insurance wouldn't cover the cost. Dr. Ongkiko gave his permission for Glenn to go by car.

Then I panicked. I didn't think that I could drive him down there by myself. I knew that Larry was going to be driving my in-laws back to Zanesville and didn't know how in the world we were going to get there. But my dear friend, Bobbie's husband, Gary assured us he would drive us down there. Van volunteered along with Shawn to go and they took the day off work to go.

This was scheduled for the day after the big snowstorm and there was still some snow on the ground. Although it was warm in October, the trees with their broken branches looked as sad as I felt. Glenn was confused and appeared old and bent over as we got him in the car. I was afraid he might have a seizure and was glad Shawn came with me. I had a tongue blade in my purse and the films from the CAT scan. I felt like a puppet and someone was moving my strings to make me react. Luckily I had a car load of people there to support me.

Gary and Van rode in the front seat with Shawn and I in the back with Glenn. He pointed at the trees like a little kid but held his head down, as if it were too heavy to hold erect. His eyes were still black and his tongue swollen, making his speech more slurred. There was something about seeing him in his red sweatsuit made me feel sadder and I just thought I couldn't get through it. Shawn reached over and grabbed my hand and I held Glenn's hand. Together we looked at the world much differently than we had ever looked at it before.

The people at the hospital were very nice and offered to let me go with him, but being claustrophobic, when I saw the MRI machine, I realized I couldn't stay and couldn't watch them put my husband into that giant tube that resembled a sewer pipe. I would trust him to their care. They smiled and went on.

We decided we would go get something to eat while we waited for him to have the MRI. Shawn and I decided we were going to look at some of the CAT scan films. We pulled the first film out of the envelope, and there was the tumor. I felt sick and wondered why I had looked. Whatever had made me want to look at that film? They gave me the final written results of the MRI and we got back in the car, ready to return to Middletown Hospital. The ride would be about forty-five minutes to an hour, depending on the traffic.

The trip back seemed faster than the one down. Glenn seemed a little more awake and responsive and we all listened as he told us what the MRI was like and how he felt being put in the tube. He entertained us well and seemed more like Glenn to me than at any other time since his seizure.

I walked him down the hall the day after the MRI to go to the shower. I still couldn't get him to let go of those britches of his. He would wrap is fingers around the elastic so tightly I was not able to undo his fingers, I became aware that someone was pushing on the door. I turned around and found Bruce and Liz. I remember the look on Bruce's face as he saw Glenn. I could see real concern there, but felt relief. I thought I could talk with him and he would help me make decisions, and understand.

I finally got Glenn's fingers pried off the elastic and he showered and washed his hair. He looked better and it was comforting to see that. He walked to the mirror when we got him back to the room and shocked himself when he looked in the mirror, seeing how bad he looked. We assured him he looked a lot better than he had a few days before.

I don't know at what point I started eating carrot cake from the snack bar, but it was about the only thing that tasted good. The chapel was across the hall from the snack bar and I would go in there and pray, sometimes several times a day. Some days I would pray three or four times, along with three or four pieces of carrot cake. This little ritual became my own quiet solace. God fed me spiritually and I ate the cake for physical strength. I knew God would answer my prayer and I also knew he was teaching me patience.

We waited and learned Dr. Ongkiko was in surgery. We wanted him to read the MRI results and tell us more. We just stood around waiting, past nine o'clock then ten o'clock, but no Dr. Ongkiko. The waiting was just about to get to me and I didn't quite know what to do. The nurses assured us Dr. Ongkiko always checked on his patients, so I knew that he would be there eventually and sure enough, we heard his footsteps in the hall. But we were in for a disappointment. He looked tired and was still in his scrubs from surgery. He had not had the time to read the MRI and told us it takes him a long time to read an MRI and we would have to wait until tomorrow.

The disappointment I felt was enormous and all I wanted to know was if this tumor was benign. My mind was screaming as I asked the Lord let that be true.

CHAPTER FOUR

The Surgery

Dr. Ongkiko did not come in early as we had hoped, and we again found ourselves waiting. The looks on everyone's faces conveyed the groups anxiety. Nurses came, Dr. Kresge came, and we were marking time till Dr. Ongkiko came. Around mid-afternoon, Dr. Ongkiko came in and confirmed he was 98% certain it was benign and would schedule surgery some time next week. I felt relief but was anxious to get surgery over with before next week. I heard him say either next Thursday or Friday. I knew I didn't want to wait that long and wanted the tumor out of Glenn's head. Dr. Ongkiko looked at me as if he had read my mind and said he was not ready to go yet, there was still too much swelling.

It's funny how the mind works at those times. You wouldn't think of wanting your husband's head cut open, but I wanted that tumor out of there. The clinical side of me knew we had to wait but I felt caught in time - we couldn't move forward, we were in limbo.

Glenn and I walked the hospital halls and cherished this time we had together. We held hands and I would kiss him, but yet I could see he had a hard time relating to me. He continued to write letters to his family, but no letter was ever addressed to me. I felt hurt wondering why, but yet I didn't want to get any letter. I was afraid he might say good-bye. We could not discuss the possibility of his death.

The one thing I did do consistently was to sneak down to the coffee shop to get coffee, and stop in the chapel. I had been there so many times, I knew exactly what that stained-glass window looked like, with the tree that was a symbol of growth helping me to learn and understand from this experience. I would kneel, on my knees and remember looking at the carpet thinking they would see my knee prints there forever. I prayed hard, but each time I walked away feeling much better. I knew the Lord would give me the strength to go on.

Suzanne stayed for awhile, then went home to take care of her family, with intentions of returning for the surgery. Life for everyone else seemed to go back to normal, except for me. Melissa went back to school and Glenn's brothers went back to work. His parents went home but my Mom and sister were there to provide support when they could. Shawn began bringing me food, and though I attempted to eat, food did not want to stay on my stomach very well.

I continued to eat carrot cake, which was the strange since I'm not a real sweets eater, but I craved the carrot cake. Sometimes I ate it three times a day, and never once did it upset my stomach.

It was during this time that I got to know the nursing staff very well. They were a young staff, not necessarily seasoned nurses. But they were all very caring and made sure I was able to spend plenty of time at Glenn's bedside. I tried to help them, too, as I knew their loads were heavy. Sometimes they would have as many as eight or nine patients to care for each morning. So I would make sure that Glenn was walked, had his shower, and that his bed was made. Very seldom did they have to do anything other than give him his meds. It was more comfortable for me to be helping Glenn and the nurses, rather than just sitting there. A couple of days I even made the bed for the patient in the next bed. It was good therapy as time marched forward.

Thursday was D-Day and my life took on a different meaning as I waited. I was frightened and scared. and my friend Bobbie and I spent every day talking. She would stop by after work and visit with me and Glenn. Suddenly it was Wednesday night, the night before surgery. I was pumped up and anxious, yet relieved. My mind was exhausted with worry and confused by the mixed emotions that the surgery had created.

The thing I remember most was going home that night, and everybody telling me to get a good night's sleep. How does a woman sleep the night before her husband has his head cut open and a tumor removed? I couldn't even focus, let alone try to sleep. Suzanne had returned and she and Bobbie sat with me at my kitchen table.

Bobbie and I, through the years, had sat there many times before. We used to sit and talk over coffee when our kids were little. We had cried together when we each lost our Dads. How our lives had changed since then, as she was now working to get her kids through school, and I was working day shift now full time, so our talks were a thing of the past. Yet here we sat talking, just like old times. Suzanne joined us. It was almost like a slumber party as we reminisced and shared funny stories. We didn't even try to sleep. It grew later and later until Bobbie announced at 1 a.m. that she had to get home.

I just sat there a while longer and finally Suzanne and I went upstairs and gave ourselves a manicure.

I knew how much she loved her brother. We remembered the old family story about the time Glenn had fed her colored crayons, and asked her if the yellow ones tasted like lemons, and the orange ones tasted like oranges. We laughed and finally looked at each other knowing we had to say our prayers and try to get a few hours of sleep. Surgery was to be early in the morning and we knew it would be a long procedure.

Interestingly enough, I did fall asleep immediately after my head hit the pillow. I remember the alarm going off and thinking it was the day we had waited for what seemed like an eternity. It had been just nine days since this had all started.

As I arrived at the hospital, I was amazed at how many people were already there. My Mom was there, people from the church, and a dear friend Rita came all the way from Dayton to sit with me. Lura and Wilbur were there, our Middletown parents. They had started out as Melissa's baby-sitters when she was in the first grade, but through the years they had become adopted in love parents. Larry came up from Zanesville to be with Suzanne, and our associate pastor, Jim Breeden, was there. He had had a car accident the night before, yet was there to sit with me. Hours. Hours.

My nerves were frazzled but the staff in surgery were wonderful. They called me when they opened his head and when they spotted the tumor. They said they would call me when the tumor was removed.

I began pacing and remember Liz being there walking with me. I don't remember what time she came, just suddenly she was there. Down the hall we walked; we walked around and around. I remember seeing the colored lines on the floor that told me how to get to x-ray and how to get to lab. I know Liz and I made small talk, but I can't remember, or did it really even make sense? I don't know.

I remember the day was almost balmy outside, a beautiful fall day and Liz took me outside. the leaves were beautiful oranges, yellows and browns. We walked around the hospital grounds. I can remember looking at my feet and the leaves thinking I was in another world or a dream.. I felt so detached from reality. But as I walked back into the waiting room, I saw friends and family. I knew they all loved me, and not one of them had left. There were a few people who came and prayed and held my hand and would leave, but most of the people stayed and supported me.

I remember when the phone rang, and they told me that the tumor was out, and that they would start closing soon. I couldn't believe it and tears of happiness and relief were so close to the surface then. It was amazing that you end up with this strength. I felt such a sense of relief, but yet still had a sense of fear because Glenn wasn't yet awake. I wondered if he would know who I was, and how long it would take him to actually wake up. It worried me if he would know people, or if he would be in some state of confusion, not realizing what was going on or what had happened.

It seemed forever, but I know it wasn't long until they called and said that he was on the way to the Recovery Room. It was at that moment I saw Bruce get up and walk through the surgery doors, returning in a moment to motion for me to come in. He was walking so fast I couldn't keep up with him and as I went by Suzanne, I grabbed her hand and she came with us.

Together we stood as they actually rolled Glenn through the Recovery Room doors from the surgery suite. I couldn't believe what I saw: his color was so pink, he looked good. His head was wrapped in the usual turban dressing, but he looked good, certainly better than he did before he went. I questioned how someone could have brain surgery and their color be better. The pressure of the tumor must have been eliminated.

They rolled him over to where the nurses were standing, and the nurses did the usual vital sign checks and neuro checks.

I heard him kind of moan, and I realized he was beginning to wake up. One of the nurses motioned for us to come over. Suzanne went to one side, I went to the other, and we each grabbed a hand. It was thrilling as he grabbed back! I assured him it was all over; we were right there and, he acknowledged us.

I couldn't believe he knew who I was. Suzanne and I asked him if he could give us a grasp, if he could wiggle his right toe, bend his left leg, all those neuro checks that we both knew so well. Sure enough, he was with us. He knew surgery was over, and was talking to us.

I turned and looked around the Recovery Room and saw Bruce had brought in Wilbur, truly my surrogate father since my own father's death a few years before. It was a moment I won't ever forget as I stood there holding Glenn's hand, and thanking God for the miracle he had created.

When I think of the history of cancer in Glenn's family I become aware of how easy it would have been for that tumor to have been malignant; or to have been inoperable, even if it was benign. But truly, the Lord had answered all of my prayers.

The nurses in the Recovery Room soon ushered us out and said that we could see Glenn again when they took him up to the Intensive Care Unit. I returned to the waiting room and everyone was standing there waiting for a report. I told them how good everything was and people began to say prayers of thanksgiving. Jim had a prayer for us and at that point I remember being overcome by an extreme fatigue. It was as if my whole body had just relaxed. We went to get something to eat and, for the very first time in days, I could taste food again, other than the carrot cake.

I stayed most of the night trying to sleep on a double chair in the waiting room. Other women were there and we began sharing the reasons we were there. One woman's husband was dying and another was like Glenn, recovering from an craniotomy. About midnight we all knelt on the floor and took turns praying. Finally Will came and encouraged me to go home and get some sleep.

I remember going home and sleeping that night for the very first time in many, many days. I didn't mean to, but I slept late as I had been used to waking up around 4:00 a.m.. As I opened my eyes, I thanked the Lord and I praised him. I called the hospital as soon as I got up, and they said Glenn was doing well. He had required very little pain medication, was coherent with stable vital signs.

I remember going into his room and seeing a worried look on the nurse's face. I didn't know what was going on, but she informed me Glenn had a little temperature. I knew Patty and felt she was an excellent nurse and trusted her. I asked what she meant by a little temp' and she said it was about 101. We both knew that a temperature of 101 wasn't too terribly alarming, that sometimes after surgery patients do develop a temp. Glenn seemed to be in good spirits, but his face had swollen. His eyes were almost totally swollen shut, and he said his head began to hurt as evening arrived.

I didn't like the way he looked as his face was flushed. Something just made me feel uneasy. Everyone had gone home except for my Mom and my sister. Glenn's brothers had come and left. Everyone assumed that the worst was over and indeed it was. Yet I knew that Glenn was hurting.

The nurses had tried to get hold of Dr. Ongkiko, but he was in surgery down at Christ Hospital in Cincinnati. Glenn's temperature was higher now at 102. He had a Tylenol order, and they gave him the Tylenol. He didn't like the shots so he had started taking his pain medicine by mouth. They were giving him Tylenol with Codeine and it had helped the pain some, but it didn't go away.

I felt more tired after my good night's sleep than I had expected, waiting to feel rested, but didn't. A fatigue seemed to set in that just didn't make a lot of sense as I stayed in the waiting room, but walked back to see Glenn every hour. He had begun to grit his teeth and it became real nerve wracking for all of us. The nurses were very nice and started letting me sit in the corner of his room. Soon my Mom came in and asked Glenn if she could sit with him a while so I could get some rest. He shook his head yes.

I knew that part of the problem resulted from the dressing being tight because of swelling. Patty came in and cut the dressing a little bit all the way around, to give him a little relief. I knew that Dr. Ongkiko was particular about his dressings, and that he usually changed all of his own.

My Mom stayed while I went downstairs, got a cup of coffee, and sat in the snack shop, watching people. Of course I had to have a piece of carrot cake. I hadn't even thought about the weight I might be putting on, but carrot cake had become my crutch. I didn't want to stay away from the room too long. I saw a neighbor there who was a gynecologist, but he looked straight through me as if he had never seen me before. I didn't know what to do and just sat there all alone.

Suddenly I remembered the little chapel and hurried to finish my coffee and scurried over there. Sure enough those marks in the carpet were from the knees. I knelt down once again and I prayed. I was still very frightened as I knew how many things could yet go wrong. In my heart I had a sense of peace, but part of me still wanted to shake and cry. Some of the things that went on in my head just didn't make sense to me, or to God I'm sure.

After I had said my prayers, I felt better and went back upstairs to Glenn's room. I went through the waiting room and spotted some of the families that I had stayed with the night before. I sat and waited to go back, my Mom and I trading places. I asked her how she felt Glenn was doing and she told me he was still gritting his teeth. She said it just made her so sad. I could tell that it was hard on her and she looked tired. My sister came and took her home and Glenn's brothers and sister came.

I waited and waited for Dr. Ongkiko. Finally, very late in the evening he arrived. Glenn's temp was now at 103, and we were more than a little concerned. The culture done of his urine was positive for an infection, probably from the Foley catheter. I learned that the Foley had gotten clamped off for awhile and he had put out over 1000 cc of urine in a very short amount of time. Since I was an ICU nurse, I knew that he didn't need a high temp, that it caused an increase in his intracranial pressure. His face was red, very swollen, and he could not get his eyes open. Dr. Ongkiko re-dressed his head and ordered antibiotics.

I decided I needed to go home for the night. My sister was working nights and I felt very comfortable that she would be there to take care of him. She didn't actually have him for a patient, but she would be there on the unit. I went in to see Glenn before I left to go home.

I thought about how many times I had gone through the hospital doors like this as a nurse on my way to work, home from work, to supper, or on my way back. It was such a strange world, but yet familiar; a world that I felt comfortable in, yet strangely uncomfortable at the same time. It was my world, a world that had been mine for over 20 years, yet I had never been on the other side. I had never had a family member in an intensive care unit before. I was scared and didn't know what to do.

As I rounded the corner into his room I could see his swollen face and the turban dressing. But the continual gritting of his teeth told me that the pain was almost unbearable. He roused and asked for a pain pill and said he just didn't think he could stand much more. I knew he had to really be hurting because he never complained. I asked him where it was hurting and he complained he couldn't take the pain in his neck. I couldn't figure out why it hurt that badly, except that perhaps they had hyper-extended his neck during surgery.

I went home about 2:00 a.m. and returned at 6:00 a.m., thinking he would begin to feel better that morning but he didn't. About 6:30 a.m. Dr. Ongkiko came in and Glenn's temperature was down to 99.8. I hoped and prayed he would begin to feel better, all of his other vital signs and neuro checks were stable. The nurses kept asking him why he wouldn't take his pain shots and he explained he couldn't stand the uncontrolled feeling the shots gave him, he preferred a pain pill. So they continued to give him the Tylenol with Codeine.

I watched the nurses come and go and they didn't seem to mind me staying with him, quietly, and watching, this world that I was so much a part of. I watched the work that they were doing, that I had done for so many years. It seemed so strange, just to sit there. I felt like I should get up and help them. I watched them pass the breakfast trays, and pick them up. I watched them pass their meds, and get the linens sorted and give baths and all the routine tasks that we do. I realized how important this work is, and how it feels to be at the other end, receiving care.

The nurse who came on day shift was named Sue, also, and I had known her for a long time. She had been my peer, and now she was my husband's nurse, and in many ways mine too. She told me to go home, get some rest, and they would take care of him. I trusted her. As I watched her I remembered the time she told the funny story about her little boy putting pussy willows in his ears and telling her his ears tickled. Lots of fun times filtered back into my brain. I knew she would take good care of Glenn and that Suzanne was there, with Melissa coming later to see her Dad.

In the afternoon we visited with Glenn. He looked better and the swelling had gone down in his face. He said the pain was a little bit better, but the way he gritted his teeth, we knew that he still hurt. The nurses continued to come on a regular basis to give him his pain medication.

There was a continual entourage in and out that evening as our pastor, church friends, and work friends stopped over. Other work friends called, and my work friends called. I had a pleasant surprise about supper time, as the pastor came from our old church, the one who had baptized Glenn many years before. I'm not sure how he heard bout Glenn being sick, but he had, and came to pray with us. The day seemed to be a week long as people came and went. I felt like I was in a box watching from a distance. I felt strange, detached, yet emotionally involved.

That evening Dr. Ongkiko popped in again, and I watched him unwrap Glenn's bandage. This time I realized that on top of his head was a very large drain. I know that the drains put into the brain are not really that large, but my perception at that particular time was that it looked like a hose going in the top of Glenn's head. I felt nauseous, my legs were weak and I couldn't get up. Patty had come in and was assisting Dr. Ongkiko as he advised us he was going to take the drain out.

I didn't want to watch and instead wanted to close my eyes, but they wouldn't close, they watched. My stomach was in my throat and all I could think about was not to throw up. Nurses aren't supposed to throw up over these things. But yet I was paralyzed. I watched everything that was happening in slow motion. There was blood, and all I could think about was that it was Glenn's blood.

I realized that Glenn didn't have any hair. Dr. Ongkiko had said he would leave some hair on the top of his head, but he was smooth shaven. I can't tell you what it was like to see Glenn without hair for the first time. I was so stunned, I don't know if it was at that moment that the reality and seriousness of all of this really hit me, or what. But the tears came, burning my cheeks. I didn't want anyone to see me crying, so I looked down real quick and stood up. I realized that my legs would hold me up, even if they were weak. I leaned out the window, as if I were looking out. I didn't want Dr. Ongkiko or

Patty to see my face. I couldn't figure out why the tears were so hot on my cheeks as I wiped them quickly, but then I realized my face was chapped from all the crying I had done.

Dr. Ongkiko was talking and telling me that Glenn was doing well. Patty was putting one of those funny surgeon caps on his head. I felt like I had parallel vision, looking at Glenn's head. I have no idea what Dr. Ongkiko said to me that day but his voice echoed in my ears. I remember saying, "Um-huh," as he walked out the door, but then wondered if many of my patients' family members said 'um-huh' when they had no idea what was being said as I just had.

I sat there with Glenn and he complained that his head and neck hurt. Dr. Ongkiko stuck his head back in the door and said, "Get him a neck pillow."

In no time Patty came in with a special pillow for his head. It had a small, little groove in it, and his head just fit in the groove . The top of it was larger, a rounded wedge shape. Almost the moment they laid his head on that pillow, he commented on the relief. They also removed his Foley catheter. He went sound asleep, didn't rouse; and slept the entire evening. His pulse rate came down and his temp returned to normal.

I sat with him, and I watched the evening shift take care of him. I had always worked three to eleven, so it seemed almost comfortable to be sitting there. Then he rolled over on his side and his surgery cap came off. I saw the incision and couldn't believe my eyes. His incision started at the very top of his head, and it looked like an upside-down hockey stick. It jagged over to the left side and down, all the way to his neck.

It was at that moment I remembered Dr. Ongkiko telling me about the tumor being very deep in between the hemispheres. He said it had a tail, and it was growing towards Glenn's left eye. It had wrapped around the optical nerve and the procedure would be a lengthy surgery of six hours.

When he gave me that information, I sort of stored it in my own brain somewhere and digested it a little bit at a time. Now these things came back to me and I again looked at the incision, remembering how he explained he was going to glue the bone flaps. My mind just couldn't accept the information then, but now the scar made it reality for me.

I became very frightened and scared, because I knew I would have to take him home soon. I knew that at some point it would just be me and him, and I wouldn't have anyone to help me. The more I thought about it, the more nervous I became. Glenn was sleeping, almost peaceful, with his new head dressing on and things were quiet. My mom was there and said she would watch him, so I decided I would go home for a little while. I wanted to try to get some rest, pull my thoughts together, check on the bills, make sure things were OK and that I hadn't missed anything. So I went home and as I walked into the empty house, it felt haunted, almost spooky.

I thought about work for the first time in days. How would I go back to work? Though the acute phase of Glenn's illness had passed, I couldn't leave him home. New questions arouse. Would I have to get home care? How much care could he give himself? I really didn't know.

As I thought about this dilemma, I knew Glenn wouldn't want to have a baby-sitter. He was already angry with me because we had put a bed alarm on him. I knew my Mom would probably be too scared to stay with him and she wouldn't know what to do, at least right away. So I decided I would play Scarlet O'Hara and think about that one tomorrow.

I went in the den and worked on some bills, checking on Melissa's college tuition, made sure the house payment had been taken out of the account like it was supposed to be, and that Glenn's checks were still being added to the account. I sat down and just sort of laid my head down on the desk and in a few short minutes I dozed off to sleep.

I didn't realize that I laid my head down for so long but it had been about an hour and a half, and the phone was ringing. I panicked with my heart in my throat as I ran to the phone. I was almost afraid to even say hello. I did so anxiously, afraid that it was the hospital calling because something had happened. But it was Melissa and, she wanted to know how her Dad was doing. We talked for a little bit, with her seeming so grown up and calm about this whole thing. She had really accepted the situation very well, as least on the surface but I wondered if she really understood it all. I really hadn't given her much attention, she had sort of been pushed in the corner somewhere. I almost forced her to go back to school. Now she was driving home for the weekend and I hoped I hadn't missed something that I should have seen, trying to meet her needs as well as mine and Glenn's.

I had so much to do, yet I had very little energy to do anything. I cleaned up and thought about some of the things people had said about me: such as how I managed to get up and put my make-up on every morning. I thought that's what Glenn would want me to do throughout this whole thing, to continue to be me. That's what I had tried to do, to take care of me because he would want me to do that. Later that evening I went back to the hospital and I was prepared to stay until the usual 1:00 a.m.

As I went back and walked down the hall that had become so familiar, I realized how funny that you come to just accept what happens. It's hard to get through, so familiar a hall, yet so different than just a hospital hallway, and yet that's what I'm most familiar with in my work. I had worked in hospitals for twenty years but as I looked at the nurses and the physicians I wondered would I ever be like them again? I went into Glenn's room. The nurses had been fantastic and didn't make me adhere to the visiting times. Glenn was sitting up eating supper. I couldn't believe how good he looked. He seemed better, and he said his head felt better, the pillow was taking all the pressure off his neck.

I looked to see what he was eating and sure enough, it was green beans and hamburger. I sort of chuckled and reminded him he been eating green beans and hamburger almost every day, except for the day they made him eat the liquid diet. He reminded me, simply, that was what he liked. We laughed with each other as truly that's all he wanted to eat, green beans and hamburger.

The night passed quickly, with friends in and out. People were there from the church, Nolan and Jim, and had words of prayer. I think everybody felt a sense of relief to see Glenn looking good. My sister and Will came by also.

Driving home I began to think about how much support the church had been to me. Their prayers had meant so much. I felt I had a one-way prayer line to God, but I also knew that there were hundreds of people in our church praying for Glenn. I wondered how I could let them know how well he was doing and began to think of how I could thank the wonderful people who had helped me through this as I dozed off to sleep. The next morning was a beautiful Sunday and it was hard to believe we had all that snow just a few days ago.

I got up and put one of my warmest sweat shirts on, because I felt cool, and my usual jeans, and I returned to the hospital. The nurses had given Glenn his bath early that morning and they had put the funny little cap on him. He said he didn't like the cap and he asked me if he could take it off. I told him he looked like he had just gotten a burr haircut, but it was really up to him, depending on how he felt.

When he took it off, I still felt the shock of seeing his head shaved with his eyebrows and mustache almost standing out on his face. He looked strange, because his head was so slick and he didn't even have a five o'clock shadow on his head.

You couldn't see the incision when you looked at him face to face and his head didn't look puffy or swollen. The drain sites were still open and there was a scab where the sutures were. All things considered, his head didn't really look bad, and he wanted to keep the cap off of his head, he didn't want anything to touch it. So we took it off and visited together a while until he dozed off to sleep.

I went back down to the waiting room and talked to some of the women I had prayed with the other night. They were in there with family and I noticed that the one lady who had been such a constant presence in the waiting room wasn't there. I asked the woman whose husband had gotten better where she was and she told me that her husband had died during the night. I couldn't believe the news and felt so sad, such a loss. We had prayed so hard that our husbands would get well, with every fiber of our body, and yet my prayer had been answered and hers wasn't. I didn't understand, felt confused, and questioned why the Lord had answered my prayer, yet her prayer had gone unanswered. I asked Him to give us understanding and tell us why these things happen.

My friend Bobby came in and we talked for a little while, going to get some coffee and my infamous carrot cake. I wondered if I was going to be Mrs. Blimpo when this was all over as the carrot cake continued to taste so good, I couldn't begin to stop. I was addicted to this carrot cake. I ate one piece, but then immediately thought I wanted another one. So I ate another one. It tasted even better than the first. At that point I really didn't even care if I was Mrs. Blimpo, somehow I would diet and get the pounds off. But right now I needed carrot cake.

I also needed my prayer time with God. I had missed church that morning. I knew that I needed some quiet time to pray. I went over to the chapel and got down on my knees. I just thanked the Lord for Glenn and I asked Him to be with the lady whose husband had died. I couldn't remember her name, but I could see her face so well as it was almost imprinted on my mind. My prayers were for her that day.

I thought how many times I had seen people die in Intensive Care, how much I cared about my patients, and how much it hurt when they died. But somehow this was different, this had a whole new dimension for me. I was different than I was a few weeks ago. It occurred to me that I had a different depth, I had become wiser. It was similar to the wisdom that came when my father died, when I knew what it was like to lose a loved one. But now I knew what it was like to walk on the other side. I knew what it was like to sit in Intensive Care to wait for surgery, to wait for nurses and physicians to give me a condition report, a ray of hope.

When I left the chapel that day, I knew that it was going to be OK and I had developed a strength I didn't know I had. When I walked back to Glenn's room, I knew I had a renewed commitment to my profession and an intense desire to let people know how important nurses are and how physicians look different from the other side. I wanted them to know the physician and the nurse really are a team, a very effective team that works together to help people overcome illnesses that are beyond any understanding.

As I rounded the corner of the waiting room, I had a smile on my face because I felt good, better than I had in days. I felt better about being a nurse than I had for the last year. The waiting room was full of our friends and family. My cousin Linda from Dayton drove down to see Glenn that day and I was amazed as they filtered in. Bruce acted as the leader, taking a group of people down to Glenn's room in ICU. I remembered there were only supposed to be two in the room at a time, but no one stopped him. Glenn was thrilled; smiling, joking and laughing about his bald head. Everyone was so ecstatic to see Glenn as his old self again.

As I watched him that day I realized that for a long time he had lost his sparkle, his humor. I thought I hadn't seen what was happening to him. I was a nurse and should have seen what was going on with my own husband, but I didn't. I had missed a very important piece in my nursing assessment. I lived with this man and yet I missed it. Some of the enthusiasm that I had felt just a few moments before began to dwindle as I began to doubt who I was. I questioned what kind of a critical care nurse would miss the symptoms of a brain tumor. I felt like I was being pulled back into a corner of the room as people came in and out and visited with Glenn.

I began remembering some of those signs and symptoms. I thought about the weekend before when we had gone to a museum with my sister and Will and the kids. Glenn seemed to take such a long time to read each little section. I had complained to him and said he had become a real slow reader. What had happened to that fast reader I knew? He had only laughed and said it seemed to take longer with age. He seemed to be having a hard time focusing all day. We came home and rented the movie 'Beaches' but Glenn couldn't seem to sit still. He would get up and pace and be sad. It was such a good story, and yet I saw he couldn't really watch it. He just paced the downstairs of the house, not really focusing on much of anything. Later, after everyone had gone, I asked him why he hadn't watched the movie and he commented that it made him sad.

I remembered at night how he would breath so irregularly. Sometimes he would have such long periods of snoring apnea that I had said to him that we were going to take him to the doctor. I remembered how dark the circles were under his eyes, and how quiet he had become. I had denied it. My Mom kept saying he didn't look good but I'd say he was just tired.

The last time Glenn and I had flown to Zanesville to visit with his Mom and Dad, I noticed that the plane was banked way over on its side. As I looked at Glenn, he had the strangest look on his face. Again on the way back, I noticed he had that same strange, staring look on his face as if he was holding the plane in a level place. He just looked like he wasn't with me. I put my arm over on his shoulder and I tried to have him respond but he didn't. He just had this odd look on his face. I shook his shoulder and asked if he were OK and he said he was fine, but he said it so mean, his voice was so deep, I was sure I had made him mad.

As these thoughts came back to me, I thought of lots of times he just didn't seem to have the attention span that he normally had. I remember Al at work telling me the day before the seizure that Glenn had been staring at a table and his face was red. Everybody in the room had thought Glenn was angry.

As I sat there thinking about all these times, of his snoring, and attention spans, I suddenly realized that someone was calling my name. I turned around and it was Shawn, who brought the kids there to see 'Daddy Glenn.' Ryan had always called him 'Daddy Glenn' because he had heard Melissa call him 'Daddy' and he just thought that was a 'Daddy Glenn'. We got a lot of strange looks when we went places, but we didn't care. To Ryan, Glenn was 'Daddy Glenn' and that's just the way it was.

Together we went back to the waiting room to get Ryan. We were trying to prepare him for 'Daddy Glenn' being in the bed, and he was so excited about going to see him. We told him he's had a needle in his arm, like you did when he was in the hospital. We told him that he had had surgery on his head, and he was fine, but that 'Daddy Glenn' didn't have any hair. He wanted to go see 'Daddy Glenn', but he didn't want to see 'Daddy Glenn' without any hair. We knew that eventually he would have to see 'Daddy Glenn' without his hair. We were ready to let him wait but then, when we started to leave the waiting room, he screamed and cried. He wanted to go see 'Daddy Glenn'. He didn't want to see him without hair, though he wanted them to put the hair back on. So we walked him back there and as we got him to the corner of Glenn's room he panicked and changed his mind

Then he caught Glenn's eye through the glass, and Glenn waved at him. He just took off towards the bed as he realized that 'Daddy Glenn' was the same 'Daddy Glenn' he had always been. He just climbed right up and gave him a big hug and kiss. It was a wonderful sight for us all to see.

I remember Kim and Rob (our good friends and ski buddies), Bruce and Liz and all those people coming in and visiting with Glenn. It was such a special time. I began to worry, though, that Glenn was getting tired as he began to look more and more tired. I worried he would get more edema. I began to worry more and more as people came in and out. It seemed that people were just coming from everywhere. I couldn't believe the nurses were putting up with this and if this were my patient, I wasn't sure I'd allow it. These thoughts kept going through my head. But I reminded myself I'm not the nurse here, and I'm not the doctor.

My cousin Linda told me she wanted to come and see the new house. Glenn had enough company and it would be good to get out for a while. It became a healing experience for me to spend time with her. We had not talked in a long time, and as I showed her the house, I felt more relaxed and comfortable.

That evening Glenn was very tired, zonked out, and I went home early. Glenn's sister called and we discussed what we might do when Glenn came home. Suzanne said she would come, take care of Glenn for the first week and was taking time off from work. She said her brother needed her, and she would be there. She relieved me of all my worries about his first week at home. I don't know if she realized how much of a help she was for me too, and how much I appreciated it. I thought about how the Lord had answered all of my prayers, every one. He was taking care of this. I wasn't doing anything, I was just along for the ride. I was learning to trust the Lord.

CHAPTER FIVE

Home Coming

On Monday morning, thirteen days after Glenn was taken ill, I went in and found him sitting up, already showered. I knew that I had to face the fact that I was going to have to take him home soon. I felt panicked inside, overwhelmed. It was all I could do to keep from running away. But how could I ran away, where would I go and I knew I didn't want to leave him. I had never felt like this before: wanting to stay and run away at the same time. I began to get a burning down inside my stomach and wondered if I would develop a stress ulcer from all of the madness. But the anxiety and frustration of so many things continued to fill up my mind. I questioned if I would be able to take care of him. I still felt like I hadn't done a very good job as a nurse, or as a wife, before diagnosis. How in the world could I take care of him now?

He was reading a book that morning and I could tell that he was on a campaign to relearn his skills of rapid reading and retention. We talked about his feelings regarding the slow thinking and I told him it was partially the medication, Dilantin, he was taking. I told him that once he got home and back to his normal routine, he would feel much better. The day passed rather uneventfully. Glenn's brothers, my sister, and my Mom came in that evening and we had a quiet visit.

Tuesday morning I woke early. It was a beautiful Fall morning and it seemed that the whole world was bustling about, trying to clean up from the snowy mess that had broken the tree branches and turned the leaves an ugly brown. Underneath you could see the fall colors coming forth. I knew it would be just a day or so and I would be taking Glenn home. The drive to the hospital seemed to be rejuvenating and I felt in good spirits as I laughed and sang to the radio. My heart was even more lifted when I saw Glenn's friendly smile and that alert look back in his eyes. I could see that he was in there again. I kissed him and he said he heard Dr. Ongkiko was coming in for early surgery due to some kind of an emergency. He was going to see his patients early. Glenn thought that he might be able to get out of the hospital. I told him that I thought maybe in the next couple of days. Glenn's deep breath indicated he wanted out of there today, and was ready to go home.

I told him I was glad he was ready, but in my mind I wasn't sure I was ready and the panic seemed to well up in me. I didn't know how to handle this one. I had never taken care of anybody at home before who had been this sick. After all, he had only been out of Intensive Care for a couple of days, not even two full days. How could they send him home?

Soon we heard Dr. Ongkiko's familiar footsteps come down the hall and his voice echoed as he came in. After asking how he felt, Glenn told him he was ready to go home. As he examined him, Dr. Ongkiko asked Glenn several questions and finally agreed he could go home. He turned toward me and indicated that a nurse, (ME), could take care of him. I sat there listening as he explained to Glenn about taking the Dilantin and the importance of compliance. He also talked how the area where he removed the tumor would develop a scar. He could seizure without the Dilantin. I felt even more frightened and as if I wanted to throw up in the trash can. But I sat there listening. I glanced at Glenn and saw a twinkle in his eye.

Glenn asked about other things. Could he do pretty much what he felt like doing? Dr. Ongkinko agreed, but cautioned against overdoing. As the conversation continued, it became obvious that Glenn was asking about sex. I wondered how they could be talking about this so soon, we can talk about sex in a couple of weeks, maybe a couple of months. Laughing, Dr. Ongkinko agreed he should do what feels good, but warned him that Dilantin sometimes causes impotence. Glenn just stared at him.

Dr. Ongkiko continued laughingly, that was why he had Glenn take it as one big dose in the evening. He would find out that it worked better that way.

So, the dismissal was written and we gathered up his things. Glenn didn't even want to stay for lunch. He wanted out of there. I could understand that and I wanted him home, but I didn't want him home. I made a few phone calls, told people that I was taking him home so they wouldn't come visiting. I called the pastor to help let the word out.

As I walked that long walk to the parking garage, I felt confused, frightened and glad at the same time. How you could be happy and scared at the same time I wasn't sure. I could see the anxiousness on Glenn's face and wondered if he, too, was a little scared. He didn't show emotion, but I knew him well enough that sometimes he just didn't express himself. I would have told him what I was feeling but he didn't say anything.

As I was driving away from the hospital I felt like I was on a first date and didn't know what to say. I felt so awkward and the silence was deafening. We made small talk about the trees and I asked him if the world looked a little different to him now that he had gone through this crisis. He admitted it did but really hadn't thought about it too much.

We got home and settled. I even managed to put together a grilled cheese sandwich and Campbell's soup for lunch. He ate, watched TV and it was good to have him home after I got over that initial fear. My Mom came over and stayed with me for awhile; with my sister stopping by. He complained about his neck hurting and I gave him two pills for his neck pain. He took a long nap, and I puttered around the house, not really knowing what to do, afraid to leave him alone even for a few seconds.

While he slept that afternoon, I thought about going back to work. I knew with my offiice-mate being let go the month before that I would be assuming more responsibilities than I had before. I questioned how I could assume more responsibilities being such a poor example of a nurse. How could I do nursing orientation for new nurses coming into our institution when I couldn't even see my husband's own symptoms. I thought of all the years I had wanted and strived to be the best nurse I could be, but failed the most important person in my life. I didn't have any recourse and there was nothing I could do. I had to learn to live with it, a tremendous feeling of failure.

I thought about the nurses who had helped Glenn and me through this madness. I wanted to somehow glorify them, because I knew there were nurses everywhere, in every institution doing the same things every day - putting their patients first and giving the very best nursing care possible. They are the catalysts that bridge from diagnosis to cure. They got the mothers through labor, support spouses through surgery, and give the needed care when no one else can. They cared. How would I recognize them? I didn't know, but somehow, some way, I would come up with something to show that nurses really do make a difference.

Glenn had a hard time watching our small portable TV, and he needed something to support his neck as he read or watched TV. I didn't know what our finances were like, I hadn't even looked at them, other than to pay the immediate bills. I knew he needed a lounge chair and a larger screen TV. So that night when I put him to bed I told him we would look for another TV and a chair that would be more comfortable. At that point I felt that we were so far into debt that a couple hundred dollars more wouldn't break us. Some things just had to be done, and he needed something to keep him quiet and entertained while he recovered.

That night he looked at me impishly as I put my gown on. I smiled, remembering Dr. Ongkiko and the earlier discussion. I agreed it had been a long time since we slept together but reminded Glenn I wasn't sure I even wanted to sleep with him after the last time. He promised not to roll out of bed or have a seizure and urged me to remember he was drugged.

He couldn't help noticing that I had moved the night stand a good foot away from his side of the bed and took the decorative pillows and padded the area between the night stand and the bed. If he rolled out his head would hit pillows instead of the floor or the corner of the night stand, but he questioned what I was doing.

I told him I had lived through it once and learned a few things. It's better to fall into something soft than to fall and hit your head on a night stand or the floor. I told him I didn't care if all the decorating books in the country say night stands should be two or three inches from the bed.

I reached for his hand and I told him I have prayed so hard for this to be behind us. I really and truly believed that the Lord had blessed us beyond our wildest imaginations and that everything was going to be OK. For the first time since all of this ordeal happened, Glenn took me in his arms and held me.

I wish I could say I felt safe, like I had before, but I didn't. I felt insecure, though I knew he was OK, but I didn't feel the security that I felt before. But it still felt good to have him snuggle me, to hold me, and kiss me again. It was a wonderful feeling. But deep down inside, I still was afraid.

I snuggled down in the bed, but I didn't want to snuggle too close. We used the hospital pillow and his regular pillows to support his head and neck. I had given him a Tylenol with codeine, hoping it would help him sleep. I laid with my head in his arms just like I had for years, with my arms around him. We snuggled and it felt good, but I was nervous and not a bit sleepy.

My Mom had said she would stay over, so she was asleep in the guest bedroom. I felt a little more secure because I had another person in the house, so if he had a seizure that I could at least get help to dial 911. We talked small talk, feeling kind of awkward, not quite knowing what to do.

I knew nothing could ever change the way I loved him. I loved him as much at that moment as I ever had but felt as if we were starting over again with a new beginning. We had been given back our lives, and were almost like newlyweds again, needing to relearn each other.

I realized they never discuss in textbooks about what to do the first night at home and in bed with your husband or wife after a craniotomy, or after a heart attack, or any illness. Nobody tells you how you're supposed to lay, how you're supposed to put your arms around them, what kind of things you can do, what kind of things can't you do. Do what you feel like doing, is what Dr. Ongkiko had said.

I wondered why someone didn't write something that tells you what to do? Was there a manual? But I knew there weren't any. So much of life is just trial and error. I just wanted to be able to sleep and to rest. I was so thankful that I had my husband here beside me, it didn't matter to me about anything, except that he was here beside me.

Glenn reached around and pulled me close, beginning to kiss me very passionately. I had been kissed like that thousands of times before, and I knew he wasn't ready to go to sleep. I objected mildly, it was his first night home, but immediately realized it had been a dumb statement to make as he professed his love and how much he missed me. I looked at his bald head, such a reminder me for and I thought I had never made love to a bald man before. Flashes of the scar on the back of his head went through my mind.

But his body was the same. He had the same furry legs that I always loved to snuggle up next to. His lips were as soft and inviting as ever. My heart raced like a bride's, but yet I was afraid. I wondered if making love would cause an increase intra cranial pressure? I'm trying to think, and all at once I felt his lips going up and down my neck, and his hands were gently fondling my breast. My protests received another rebuttal as he reminded me he had been away from me too long.

I was sure somewhere there's an article, a chapter, something I can read as to what I'm supposed to do and I wanted to cry. Tears started streaming down my face. I tried not to let him see, as I wiped them into the pillow, but he kept kissing me. Suddenly I felt his body hard against mine and realized he wasn't impotent. He grinned that sheepish grin of his and assured me there was nothing to worry about. The Lord has just taken care of everything.

I was surprised that my own body could even come back to life again, it had felt so numb for weeks. I had totally put that part of my life out of my mind, out of my memory. I was surprised by how easily my body remembered, how quickly it responded to his touch. I think fear enhanced our passion and our lovemaking.

I felt wonderful as I lay there in Glenn's arms. I didn't know how many moments that we would have, if our time would be limited. But I was thankful for this time, this time that we had together. Words really can't describe the feelings that I had. I also knew deep down inside that God had promised me to have faith in Him, and that He would take care of us. That He had a purpose and a plan for Glenn's life and for mine. I didn't know what that plan would be, but I knew that I was beginning to develop a new strength and courage.

On Sunday I thanked our church for all their prayers and for their concerns and all the many cards and flowers. I told them just how important prayer is in a person's life when they go through a crisis like this. God is truly the only one that can get us through, and it's the prayers of His people that support us along these hard ways that life deals us.

CHAPTER SIX

The Tulips Bloom

Suzanne arrived to take care of Glenn the first week he was home. They spent many hours remembering their childhood. They watched old Agatha Christie movies, read books, and went to department stores and discount stores. They had a good time, visiting with each other and getting to know each other again as adults. It was a nice thing for me to watch.

Work is a funny thing. I had been gone for four weeks. The first day back my desk was piled high, but yet I slipped back into the groove very quickly. I still had that sense of maybe not being the best nurse that I could be, but that had sort of been pushed aside. I felt more determined to do something with my work that would help in some small way to display what nursing care had meant to both of us. I also wanted to share with others what nursing meant to me.

It was a pretty hard order to fill as a nursing educator who suddenly finds herself thrust into extra responsibilities because of cutbacks in the department. Doing your job and someone else's is always difficult. It seemed like everywhere I turned, there was more work, more things to be done, more proposals to be written, more people to be educated, more people wanting this and wanting that. Use of forms were the big thing, and the question was how to educate nurses to do them?

I had a good friend, Don who sat with me one afternoon and came up with an idea of doing it on video. It came to fruition as we knew we would use the story about Glenn. We would use his admission to the hospital, his nursing assessment, and how they continued to assess him both pre-and post-op. It became a real challenge for us to see if we could actually pull it off and we did.

One afternoon Glenn came to the hospital and we wrapped his head up, put eye shadow underneath his eyes to depict those black eyes that he had and even darker eye shadow to depict the bruises that he had all over his body. Then we video-taped. It took us several hours, but it was very realistic. We had enough segments that we could use and an actual video script. Don and I worked long hours and days putting all the pieces together. The video even had a really unique ending.

Glenn sat on the corner of the window seat at the hospital and talked about how much his nurses meant to him, and how much their care and kindness had meant. He also discussed how they had helped me during this time of crisis. It was unique because we used the video for nursing orientation, and it would eventually be shown to every nurse in the institution. We were very proud of our video and felt we had a good product. It gave recognition to nurses everywhere for the great job that they do and I felt I had achieved an important goal for myself.

Melissa came home for Christmas that year, seemed down and very despondent, not her usual self. I thought maybe it was because of all the things she had been through. But her second day home she confided that her grades were not going to be very good this year. I was heartsick, but knew that she had been through a lot, so we didn't ride her too much. Sure enough, her grades came and she had a D in English. As freshman English is pretty hard, we advised her to take it again. She would do better and have a better second semester.

Somehow we managed to have Christmas gifts for everybody. Melissa wanted to put the Christmas tree in our dining room in front of the bay window, and we did. It was a beautiful tree, although it was the same tree that we had been using for twenty years. It was still the most beautiful Christmas tree we had ever had as it seemed to be the symbol that love can endure. I knew that God's love for us had truly displayed itself in these last few weeks.

Christmas was a time to re-adjust our values. We didn't have much money. Glenn had asked me what I wanted for Christmas, and I told him all I wanted was a set of glasses that went with my everyday dishes. Sure enough, under the Christmas tree, a few days before Christmas, were the two square brightly wrapped boxes. I was happy and content. I couldn't have asked for anything because I had Glenn there, alive, healthy, wonderful. I would tease him because his head was still so very bald, but tell him when the tulips bloomed he would have hair again. Then we would laugh.

Glenn was going back to work part time, and with some full time days, and doing pretty well. It was a few weeks before Christmas when he got a phone call. It was from one of the organizations at the base where he worked, and they wanted him to come and interview for a job. He called me at work and asked if he should go and make the extra effort. He had been to several of these interviews and really hadn't had anything materialize. Here he was with no hair, and just getting over this brain tumor. What did I think? I urged him to go or risk always saying to himself, maybe he should have. That way people would know he was still interested next spring if something else came up. He did go and that evening when we came home, I asked how the interview went.

He commented that it was pretty short and they didn't say too much. He had just answered their questions and didn't even ask them any questions. Usually Glenn does ask lots of questions, but this time didn't, just thanked them and got up and left. He added he didn't think he had all the requirements they wanted for the job. I reassured him he had the stuff he needed and I didn't care of he ever got another promotion.

Glenn and I seemed to grow closer together, more so than before the tumor, before surgery. A deeper bond began to develop and we leaned on each other and learned to pray together. Every night at bedtime we would sit down, hold hands and pray.

Christmas day came, although cloudy like it always is in Ohio. My Mom stayed over and we all sat out in the dining room underneath the tree and unwrapped our packages. We all had a good time, laughing and playing with out toys. I picked up one of my two packages and Glenn told me to open the one he held in his hands. I picked up the second package, they both looked alike. But Glenn urged me to open the one he held.

So, I opened the "special" box and noticed in one of the small glasses was a little square velvet box. When I said the usual, 'you shouldn't have,' Glenn said I deserved something special since in a few days I would be married to this bald man for twenty years.

I very shyly opened up the box and couldn't believe what I saw, the most beautiful sapphire and diamond ring I had ever laid eyes on. It was a band like ring and it wasn't real fancy, but it was beautiful. I put it on my right hand even though it was a little big. As he held my hand, Glenn remarked that the ring was for twenty years of continuous service, and for saving his life. He thought I deserved something.

I felt kind of like a schoolgirl getting a gift, very shy, and not quite knowing what to do. I took off my wedding bands and put the new one back on, holding it in place with my wedding bands. As I did that, it looked so pretty I thought I would have it cut to fit my left hand and wear it here. It was a symbol of our second twenty years together, of a new beginning. We could be happy to have this time together, with this ring a symbol of our new beginning. I kissed him.

Melissa and Mom were watching this and acting embarrassed and silly. Mom and I cooked a big turkey dinner and Shawn, Will and the kids came over. We took pictures and it was a quiet Christmas, but a Christmas I'd always remember.

After the holidays we sent Melissa back to school and it was different this time. As I reflected back, I didn't cry and feel as sad like I had before. This time I looked forward to the time that Glenn and I would have alone. We got used to driving back and forth to work together, discussing work and talking about each other's days. Some days we would cook, and some days we would stop and eat some place on the way home. Life settled into a pattern that seemed very comfortable.

Seven o'clock in the evening was Glenn's down time. Somehow we had managed to buy a couple of recliner chairs and a larger screen TV so we could see TV across the family room. We spent a lot of time watching Wheel of Fortune and Jeopardy. It was a challenge to our brains, as we tried to answer the questions on Jeopardy, and to solve the phrases on the big wheel. It became a very pleasant routine.

I'm sure that many people would think our life was very boring, but our life was anything but boring. We had two very demanding jobs. The interview had gone better than Glenn thought and they hired him the first of the year. We couldn't believe it, because it meant a big promotion and a sizable amount of money. Once again the Lord had provided for us. He had given us the extra money so we could pay off the doctors and hospital bills.

The hospital bill was pretty phenomenal. We couldn't really believe how much it had cost. Dr. Ongkiko had given me a professional discount even though I didn't work in that hospital and had never worked for him. However, the other bills, the unforeseen bills that people never think about began to mount. It seemed like every time we turned around somebody was charging us for something. But we managed to make it. We watched what we bought, watched what we ate. We didn't buy anything frivolous, and kept managing to pay for Melissa's schooling.

We heard from her frequently when she first went back to school, but pretty soon we didn't hear from her as often. She had met some new friends, a girl named Cathy, a fellow named Bill and a another, believe it or not, that she had gone to kindergarten with, way up in northern Dayton, a young man named Rick. The four of them had just become a real gang and I could tell from her letters and her phone calls they did everything together.

She was having a good time, and was pledging to a sorority, Alpha XI Delta. She knew all the Greek alphabet, but deep down inside I was hoping she was remembering some English. But she was twenty, I had to let go and I couldn't mother her the same way anymore. I couldn't lay out her clothes to go to school and certainly couldn't tell her how hard to study. She knew it was her responsibility. She was learning to stand on her own and Glenn and I prayed, hoping she was learning how to study and be a responsible adult.

March came and we watched our friends prepare to go skiing. Glenn and I had taken up skiing about five years before, but we knew we wouldn't be able to ski this year. We watched them leave the first of April to go to Vail, Colorado. Glenn and I had skied Utah a few years before, but we had never skied in Vail. They sent a video back, waving and telling us how much they had missed us, almost as much as we had missed them. We moped around the house, but then it dawned on us just how lucky we were and we stopped moping and went window shopping.

Glenn had no signs of seizure activity. The only thing that plagued us at all, throughout his healing process, was that he still jerked at night. His whole body would do this, sometimes violently. His arms and legs would jerk, and sometimes his legs would almost knock me out of bed. I often woke up more tired than when I went to bed. But so many good things were happening, I tried to put it aside and not think about it. The doctor said it was part of the reaction to the Dilantin and that it would eventually subside.

When the Tulips bloomed in April Glenn had hair! His head was covered with a short fine red hair. He began to look more and more like Glenn, the one I knew when we first met. His hair was totally overgrowing the big, wide incision that went down the back of his head. I know that he felt more comfortable with himself, and I did too. I would tease him. I had gotten comfortable making love to a bald headed man.

Our friends came back from Vail and shared their experiences with us. We enjoyed watching the video of them almost as much as if we had gone. Spring came and I felt more at peace, more comfortable.

Our Ladies Sunday School class at church had been dwindling in size and the church had asked me if I would think about taking it over full time in the fall. I told them I would think about it, but didn't know how I would be as a full time teacher. But if the Lord wanted me to do that, I thought, I will.

It was almost time for Melissa to come home and the time had gone fast. I wondered how her grades were as we hadn't heard anything about grades, all we had heard about was her new friends and the fun things that they were doing. I had these little worried feelings deep down inside, like a lot of mothers, but I just kept them to myself. She came home with lots of dirty clothes, like all college students do, and moved in again with a bang. We had to pack things away in the basement not knowing where she got all this stuff. It was fun, moving her back home.

After she got home, she casually told us that she didn't do well in English again. But her other grades weren't bad, so we had hopes of pulling her through. I told her she would have to go to summer school to get through English. Defiance had said that she could take English in the fall. I realized she tried it twice there and didn't make it. There was something wrong. I wanted to see some of her papers so she gave me the name of her instructor to call and see if I could get her to send a couple of the papers to find out what was going on. We needed to make a decision as to whether to send her to summer school or not. After all, it meant extra money that we really hadn't anticipated.

I called the instructor and she was very nice agreeing to send the second paper the Melissa wrote. She had been given chances to write the paper and claimed to have written all of those "helpful hints" for her to improve.

A few days later the paper came in the mail. When I opened it and read it, I found there were only three "helpful comments" written on that paper. I knew a run on sentence when I saw one, I understood themes, and I certainly understood about writing papers after wading through a Master's theses. I picked up that paper and all it said was, "One run on sentence in the beginning paragraph." "Theme," was written at the top and something about the body that I couldn't understand. I thought that if these comments were intended to help her with the paper, I certainly didn't see it. So I called the instructor back and she got a little bit huffy with me as she described how she had helped Melissa.

As I hung up I thought maybe she did help her, but it certainly wasn't evident in her comments on the paper.

I called Miami, got a schedule for English, got the paperwork, and sent Melissa over there. She really liked her instructor even though she was not a happy camper about going to summer school. She did well on the very first paper she wrote, an A, and really bonded with this instructor. I began to think maybe our worries will be over. She actually had a good time and she smiled more than I had seen for a long time. It was a good summer, we all had a good time, even though we didn't have money to go on any big vacations, we spent time visiting with our family. We had picnics, even a big one on the Fourth of July in the backyard. Life was good.

In the fall, Melissa went back to school though I didn't really want her to go back to Defiance I wanted her to go to Main Campus at Miami and a little feeling of worry began to grow inside of me. But Glenn and Melissa both wanted her to go back to Definace and this tiny feeling inside kept gnawing at me. The closer the time came for her to go to school, the more panicky I felt. I didn't want my daughter going back to that school. When we had a family vote, it was still two to one. Melissa was going back to Definace. Glenn felt she needed to be away from home.

We packed her up, and sent her back. We got to school early and her friend, Rick, met us in the hallway. He was a nice looking young man. He had sandy brown hair and was about the size of Glenn. You could tell that he really liked Melissa. He was very polite and nice. He helped take Melissa's TV cabinet to her room and he carried things from our car to her room. When we left campus they were siting, talking, and I realized that was one of the reasons she wanted to go back. He seemed like such a nice young man.

All the way home I thought about Melissa, turning into a very beautiful young woman. It was time for me to think about letting go of her. Someday she would be getting married and leave home. This is a natural progression, I told myself. But all the talk in the world didn't make that uncomfortable feeling deep down inside go away, it stayed. Even the first few phone calls, the first few letters, didn't' make it go away.

Glenn had his yearly CAT scan in October, and the results were good with no problems. Dr. Ongkiko sat and talked to us and asked us all kinds of questions. We talked about the jerking that he did so much at night and he told us that sometimes happened.

He asked if it was getting better or worse and we said it's just still there. He just sort of shrugged. What could we do? We couldn't take him off the Dilantin and he was doing well otherwise. Glenn seemed brighter and his thinking and math abilities seemed to be returning to normal. Maybe our hours of watching Jeopardy and Wheel of Fortune were beginning to pay off.

Melissa on the other hand, seemed to grow quiet, almost despondent at times. She seemed sad. I called her a couple of times and she almost cried. I would ask her what was the matter and she would respond, nothing I began to notice that the group had become a threesome instead of a foursome. That it was just Bill, Cathy and Melissa.

One time after a short conversation, I turned right around and called her back. I knew she had to be in her room, because I had just talked to her. The phone rang and rang and rang. Finally she answered and I asked what had happened? What happened to Rick? Did she and Rick break up, and what was going on?

She informed me they had never truly been going together, but were just friends.

I knew, there was something wrong there and asked, when you have a foursome like that, surely he didn't break up with all three of them. Melissa told me that Rick wasn't like the rest of them, he had told her he was a homosexual.

I was flabbergasted and couldn't believe it. This nice young man that had stood there beside Glenn. What happened? What happened to him? I was just totally and completely stunned. I told her that I was sorry, and that I really hadn't wanted to pry. But maybe she would feel better now that she had told us, and we would understand a little bit why it was just the three of them.

Melissa admitted it did help a little bit to talk about it as they all missed him and were good friends. I told her I loved her and would support her, reminding her to study hard, and we would visit for her birthday.

After that Glenn and I felt that it would be a good idea to go ahead and maybe try to scrounge a little money for a new coat. Her's was looking pretty bad. We'd take her a cake, and share it with Cathy and Bill. So the next few weeks were spent planning Melissa's birthday. We took Mom and my nephew Ryan up with us.

It was a beautiful fall morning and even though it was November, you really didn't need anything but a sweat shirt or a sweater. The campus was beautiful. The leaves had fallen, but yet still some of them were still clinging to the trees.

When we went to Melissa's dorm, and she showed us her room, I was amazed at how neat and clean it was. It was cleaner and neater than most of the rooms. She had done a nice job, and I told her so. We met Cathy and Bill in the big reception room where the piano was and Melissa said she had been playing again. That excited me because I always loved to hear her play. We had the cake, and took her out to eat. I could tell that they all felt somebody or something was missing.

They said they were going to come down and visit with us in a few days, that Melissa wanted to show Cathy and Bill Middletown which was fine with Glenn. We took

Melissa out to eat, then went to a mall. We got her the new coat, took her back to the campus, and then drove home.

I felt better about taking her back to school that day than I had for a long time. I even slept better that night than I had. The little feeling I had deep down inside hadn't totally gone away, but it seemed a little softer since I had met Bill and Cathy. They seemed like such nice kids. They both had good grades, Bill with almost a 4.0, and Cathy had a 3. something.

The next few weeks, I seemed to talk a lot to Melissa. She began to talk a lot about Bill and that they had done this or that. I thought maybe they would become the next twosome. She said Bill lived off-campus in an apartment, and the three of them spent a lot of time there watching videos. Again, I began to get that uneasy feeling and I hoped she was studying.

Mid-term grades came on a Thursday, and I was just astounded. Her grades were terrible with a C, two D's and an F. I couldn't believe my eyes and I was mortified. I tried calling, and calling. She wasn't in her room, wasn't on campus, and nobody knew where she was. I called up midnight, and still didn't get an answer. I left messages on her answering machine, and at the main desk. I couldn't find her. I felt panicky, and Glenn and I thought maybe we'd have to cancel work and drive up the next morning. I decided I would try to get Bill's phone number and got it from the main desk. I called there and he gave me a number where I could find her. Finally she returned my calls, saying she knew why I was calling. She knew I had her grades and would be mad. She also knew I would make her come home.

I assured her I just wanted to know what was going on, and if she was OK. Melissa cried and said she felt terrible. She couldn't believe she got such bad grades. She couldn't believe she had failed.

I tried to reason with her and let Glenn talk to her, but we both hung up feeling worse. It was one o'clock in the morning and I felt sick all over. We didn't know what to do. We laid awake, holding each other. We finally got up, drove to work, and went through the motions of work that day.

I had applied for a new position as a Clinical Nurse Specialist for Critical Care. My new boss came and told me that day I had the position if I wanted it. It was one I had always wanted, but my mind was on Melissa. A lot of the excitement that I wanted to feel about my new position was lost. I accepted the position, with a very guarded and sad heart. All my thoughts were centered on what we were going to do with Melissa and her grades.

CHAPTER SEVEN

My New Job

The new job was one of the first Clinical Nurse Specialist positions in the institution in which I was employed. There had been two other positions, one in ER and one in the geriatric unit. but they only had been filled for a year. I truly hoped that I could make this position have some usefulness to the institution. It was going to be a real challenge.

I soon found out that there were people who had some real negative feelings about me accepting the position. One of the nurse managers of the critical care units told me that I would have to prove myself to her and her staff. I really felt very sad about that, because I really liked this nurse manager, and wanted her support. I felt taken aback by her cold response, that I would have to prove myself. I realized that the staff in the units had never seen me in a clinical role, but I had over seventeen years as a critical care nurse.

I had managed to deal with the feelings that I had about Glenn's symptoms. I realized how very clouded his symptoms had been, that they would have been hard for anyone to pick up. Even a physician would not have been able to see the few symptoms that Glenn had displayed prior to his tumor. So I didn't really understand this response, that I wasn't a clinical nurse.

However, I started out with enthusiasm, knowing I had the full support of my new manager. She was excited, and made me feel excited. I was ready to do something different. I had enjoyed doing nursing orientation and education, but needed a change, something different. I was so tired of doing the same thing and nursing orientation is doing the same program month after month. That just wasn't me. Now I needed change, and this offered me that opportunity.

I was to accept my new position on December 15th. I went to both a Christmas party in the old office and a Christmas party in the new office. It was fun, and I enjoyed the challenge of meeting new people and making new friends, but I also felt sad about leaving old friends. My former manager was one of the very best managers I had ever had in my career, and I knew I would miss her friendship. I had felt very close to her in the four and a half years we had worked together. I appreciated all the good things we had learned from each other but also knew she was the kind of person I would probably never hear from again. She, too, was leaving the institution, going to a new place and a new position. I knew I would miss her, but life has its endings and its beginnings, and so I jumped on the bandwagon of new beginnings.

Melissa would be coming home in a few days and knew that if her grades weren't better, she would have to come home for good. I could tell in the last few weeks she had buckled down and was really studying hard. Every time we called the dorm, she was in there studying, or she was at Bill's apartment, with Cathy, studying. They too jumped in and studied with her. They had come home briefly one weekend and talked to us about how they were helping Melissa study. We had hopes that she would be able to pull it out. The feeling that I felt deep down inside was still there, but maybe a little smaller. One night after devotion, I told Glenn about this feeling. I shared with him this feeling of uneasiness, but we didn't know what to say or what to do about it. I figured only time would make it go away.

Melissa had been voted by her sorority to represent them at a Defiance Beauty Pageant. She called and wanted us to come up. So Glenn and I drove up on a Tuesday. Cathy met us at the auditorium door and showed us to our seats. She was quiet and seemed distant and preoccupied. She said Melissa was backstage and would meet us at the end of the pageant.

Melissa played the piano for her talent and wore a black formal for the competition. She looked beautiful, but didn't place. She seemed happy as she met us and talked about her fear of stumbling over her high heels. She was in good spirits and claimed to have been studying hard.

All at once the holidays were upon us. It was a good holiday season. We had a little bit more money than we had ever had for Christmas. There were no illnesses hanging over our heads and it was a great, fun time. Everybody got together at my mother-in-law's house, just like old times. We unwrapped gifts, a very, very special Christmas.

Glenn and I went out on our anniversary of twenty-one years. It didn't seem possible. I was happier than I had been twenty-one years before. It was amazing that so many marriages ended in divorce, because our marriage seemed to be growing stronger, and we were growing closer. Every moment was precious to us, everything that we did was a special time. It was like we were keeping score of all the good times.

We only had one bad thing that seemed to plague us at that time, Glenn's jerking at night. It really seemed to be wearing on my energy level and I was very tired. I couldn't quite figure out what to do about it, and kept wondering if I could just get a couple of good nights sleep at some point.

Melissa came home, and we could tell that she was not happy. She said she felt she did well on a couple of her tests, but one she was very concerned about. I'll never forget that fateful day the grades arrived. Her anger was high, she was mad, angry, and so hostile. She screamed, cried, and slammed doors, Glenn and I felt we had to live up to what we had said, that she had to come home, that we couldn't afford to continue to send her to school. She had known that the whole semester long, and yet her grades were terrible.

We told her we had promised her four years of an education, and would live up to that promise. But the rest of the time would have to be here at Miami. We told her if she did well, and we didn't have any more horrendous bills, that we would send her to the main campus after a semester or two at our local campus here. She came home very begrudgingly.

During the holidays we had gotten a couple of notices from her bank that said she had bounced a check. It was a small amount, $15, no big deal, but the fee was exorbitant, $60 for writing a bad check. I told her it was a good lesson to learn but she said she didn't remember writing the check at all.

I told her sometimes we do forget about things like this, but felt like I was walking on eggshells. Her emotions had been so up and down.

A few days later another check bounced and again she came to me and said she didn't write the check. Again a few days later another check and then a couple more. It seemed like every day checks were bouncing, and even at places Melissa didn't shop.

Then I began to have my doubts and began to wonder what in the world was going on. The nursing part of me became analytical, kids who don't do well in school, have violent mad attacks, sometimes they end up on drugs. I was scared, and frightened she might be on drugs. I denied it, I didn't even want to look at her. But one day she came in, she had been out working on some projects, trying to figure out where these checks were coming from. I looked at her, her eyes were clear, pupils weren't dilated and her arms were clean. She didn't look like a druggie. I looked at her nose as best I could to see if maybe she was doing coke. I wanted to be discreet about my assessment of her and didn't know what else to do.

I went on to work, and at lunch that day with my manager she asked what was wrong. I confided in her that I was worried about my daughter, about the bad checks, and her mood swings. One afternoon a few days later, I was sitting at my desk when Melissa called. She was hysterical and crying. It seemed that the Defiance Police Department had been investigating the check bouncing. They had all her bounced checks in their possession. Melissa called her friend Cathy to tell her the awful thing that was happening. She couldn't imagine who in the world would be doing such a terrible thing to her. Cathy sympathized and empathized with her. Melissa also told Cathy that she wouldn't be coming back to school after the first of the year. I don't think Cathy and Bill were surprised by the fact that Melissa wouldn't be returning to school.

The beginning of January, Melissa took the little car her grandmother had given her and drove up to Defiance. I had gone to work that day but had a terrible headache that I was attributing to stress. As the day wore on, I felt worse and worse. I had taken enough Nuprin to fill a battleship, but without any relief. Glenn called me about noontime and said that we were going to have to drive up to Defiance as Melissa had called and said she couldn't get all her things in the car. We would have to go help her. I had plenty of extra hours that week, so I didn't really worry about leaving early. I went to nursing service, told my manager, and left. I gave her a little rundown of what had happened with Melissa and schooling. She was always so very understanding and told me to go ahead and leave.

My head was pounding as I walked out into the cold, brisk air. The longer I stood there, the worse it got but in just a few minutes Glenn rolled up. I jumped in the car and away we went. We were just north of Dayton when I told Glenn to stop the car, that I was going to be sick. I was wearing just a sweater and skirt because I had been so warm in the car. As I got out of the car, the cold air hit me, but it didn't help. I was still nauseated, and I threw up along the side of the road. I imagined the people going by probably thought I was drunk, throwing up along the highway. I got back in the car and thought I would get some relief after throwing up like that. There was no relief and the pain continued. We had gone too far for Glenn to turn around and had to have her out of the dorm at a certain time. We were on a pretty short time frame to even get there and help her. We sped on. A little further along it happened again. This time when he stopped I hung my head over a big silver guardrail and projectile vomited all over the side of the hill. I felt embarrassed as cars drove by. I knew people thought I was drunk, but also, maybe they would be glad I had a designated driver and wasn't behind the wheel.

I got back in the car, and drifted in and out of sleep. Glenn stopped and got me a 7-Up, and I took a couple more Nuprin, and was able to rest for a little bit. I really didn't even realize we were in Defiance when I woke up. Glenn told me to stay in the car, and he helped Melissa pack. Melissa gave me one of her pillows to sleep on. It felt good and I didn't even try to help them. I remember very little about driving back.

When we got into town, I told Glenn to take me straight to the hospital, I couldn't stand the pain any longer. I continued to have dry heaves, there was nothing more in my stomach. Thankfully I didn't have to wait long in the Emergency Room. One of the physicians said he thought it was a severe migraine. I couldn't ever remember having a headache like this. I couldn't stand any light, and just wanted to keep my eyes covered. All the doctor did was give me a shot and tell me to see my doctor the next morning.

The shot did ease the pain and I felt a little better when I woke up the next morning, but I couldn't go into work. Glenn offered to stay home and take me to the doctor, but I was sure Melissa would take me. I drifted back off to sleep, still in that drugged state. I woke up about 9:15 a.m. and tried to call the doctor. Dear Dr. Kresge had passed away with leukemia just a few months before after nine years in remission. His associate was too busy to see me and couldn't get me in till the next Tuesday. I tried to explain to them that I had been very ill the night before, and had been in the Emergency Room, but it didn't make any difference to them.

So I began calling doctors at random. I realized I was going to need a new physician. I felt that I needed someone who cared about me. Finally I found a physician who was taking new patients. That afternoon Melissa took me and I met my new physician face to face. I had met him a few times before, because I had worked in the local hospital and we had seen each other, but I didn't really know him. He was nice and seemed concerned. I like him and decided that I would continue to go to him, and have my records transferred there. I spent most of that day in a drugged state. He gave me Tylenol #3s, and I stayed in the dark until the pain finally more or less wore itself out.

I went back to work the next day and things were as usual. It was a busy time, trying to get the new position in place. My new supervisor had wanted me to put together some orientation materials and to get ready to do competency testing for our critical care nurses. I was chairing the policy and procedure committee and getting to know the nurses on the units, trying to have them begin to see me in a clinical role. I made daily rounds at first, helping whenever I could. There were still those that were skeptical out there. Some of the nurses on the units would run into their patient's rooms and not even talk to me. It felt strange when I would see them get up and leave, but I was bound and determined to put the position together and felt supported by our administration and especially my new manager.

One afternoon after rounds Melissa called and asked me to come home. She was crying, almost hysterically, and told me they had found the person who has been writing the bad checks. My heart just stopped, but I managed to ask who it was. She said it had been Cathy stealing the checks and writing them against her name. Melissa began sobbing even louder into the phone. I told her I would be home as soon as I could and immediately called Glenn to tell him that Cathy had been responsible for this mess. I left as quickly as possible to go home and try to help Melissa through this.

As I drove home, my mind went from one thought to another, realizing how we all had trusted this girl. Yet relief flooded through me that it wasn't Melissa, that she was truly an innocent bystander in this. I didn't really know what I would say when I got home, but I prayed and asked the Lord to give me the words to speak, and He would know what would be best for me to do and to say. When I opened the door, Melissa came running. It was almost like she was a little girl again, she cried and put her arms around me. I could see that she couldn't believe that someone would betray her so, and my heart just went out to her. These are the things you want to protect your kids from but often can't. Sometimes we just have to give support and love when we see our children hurt by the world.

Melissa was angry, and she yelled. She wanted to go to Defiance and confront Cathy, but was scared, and didn't know how to handle it. We talked for a long time, and together we started cooking supper. By the time Glenn came home, we had a nice meal fixed. It was good that the two of us were able to be on the same wavelength, fixing supper, and almost joking at times about different things as we cooked. We all felt relief. At least now we knew the truth and could deal with it.

I felt tired after supper and laid down on the sofa falling into a fitful sleep. I slept for a long time and woke in time to go to bed. Melissa stayed up most of the night, wandering around the house. Every time I would wake up, I would hear her walking around. The TV would be on in her room, or she would be walking. I had to go to work the next day and invited her to join me for lunch. But she had classes, and couldn't do that. I was glad that she was in school as it kept her mind focused on other things. After this incident I began to see her pull into a shell. I prayed that with time she would be able to let go, and be happy. This wasn't something she would get over in a few short weeks.

It was close to the time that we would usually go skiing with our friends, and we wondered if we could really get the money together to do it. We kept saying yes, we would go, but we really didn't know where the money would come from. We had been saving, and I had a little bit of money put aside but it was expensive. We decided that we would take Melissa with us and make this a family vacation, one we could enjoy as a family. After what we had been through, we felt we needed some fun time together.

I decided I would go on a big exercise kick and try to get my legs in shape for skiing, as it had been almost two years since we had skied. I would come home and exercise, but I would be so tired. I'd go to sleep on the sofa and pretty soon my exercising became less and less and I slept more an more. I kept talking about my bone tiredness. I thought it was because I was pushing so hard at work. I had been puting in extremely long hours. I would go in as early as seven and work till six or seven in the evening. I was working on learning packets and booklets for the nurses to study for their competency testing. I couldn't understand why I felt so tired and kept thinking it was being 44 and getting old. I hated being so tired.

I also had been having some problems with my stomach, which I attributed to nerves. I went in to my doctor, told him that I was having diarrhea, and hadn't really felt good since I had had that severe headache in January. I asked him if he could give me something to settle my stomach, and figure out why I was so tired. He said I probably just need a good vacation. When I told him that we were going skiing, he said that's what the doctor ordered. I took the medicine for my stomach, and told myself I felt better. It wasn't long till we would be skiing, and we would have a good time, I was sure.

CHAPTER EIGHT

Bone Tired

The ski trip was only a few weeks away and we were cleaning skies and ski boots. The three of us were excited and happy about the trip. Melissa would be driving, and the rest of us would be flying in Bruce's plane. The day dawned early and we were ready.

I loved to fly and was excited, I had always had a secret desire to learn to fly. However, our trip was somewhat marred by engine problems on the way to Vail. We had to make an emergency landing when something went wrong with the engine. We ended up walking around an airport in the middle of Kansas while they worked on the plane. The week went much too fast but we did have a good time.

The only thing that was difficult for me was my tiredness. I didn't seem to have the stamina, I usually had. I attributed it to being away from skiing and exercising and dealing with all the stress that had gone on in our lives in the last couple of years. But, nonetheless, we had a good time, and had some great memories to bring back. I didn't break any bones and came back feeling much more like a family, a great time with Christian friends.

It was busy at work when I got back from the skiing trip and it seemed like things took off. Events were happening so quickly at work that I didn't really have time to even stop and think. But the fatigue continued to plague me. Finally one day my mom commented that every time she called she would wake me up. I began to think about the fact that it did seem that I was always asleep on the sofa, but again attributed it to long hours at work and getting ready for those workshops that we've put together. The process of putting the materials together was very demanding.

The summer days passed quickly as I learned more about my job and began filling in for staff when some of the units had call-ins. I enjoyed being back at the bedside and I was enjoying seeing the booklets come together. We had put together a workshop to simulate the competency testing format, a trial run. It was a lot of work, but I knew it would assist our nurses and help them through a rather stressful situation.

We were just a few weeks away from the workshop. I'd put together a book on pacemakers and a clinical checklist booklet. We were ready to practice the stations for the workshop but I was so tired, I could hardly go. It was hard for me to continue the pace and tried I to work more reasonable hours as the time came closer. The assistant nurse managers and the nurse managers were busy and everybody was in a state of denial about competency testing. Nobody really wanted to face the fact that it was going to be happening in just a few months. So I ended up spending more and more hours at work.

I had became very good friends with my office mate, Diane who was as short I was. We would confide in each other and even went shopping together at a petite store. We would often have lunch together with friends, as the Lunch Bunch, and have "booth talks" in the cafeteria. Daine was really the one person that was holding me together at that point, because I felt depressed about the way some of the nurses continued to treat me. Some of them still expected me to prove myself and got up and left when I came on a unit.

I was nonetheless proud of the work I had done and the things that I was doing, but it was hard, and I was so tired. I really felt as if fighting the fatigue might be making me depressed, or I was just working too hard. The week before the workshops I put in long hours, adding the final touches. I worked with the vendors for some of the new equipment, and set up snacks with fresh fruits and different kinds of healthy rolls, muffins, and other foods for the nurses as they went through the various stations. I even made the signs.

My manager came down and explained some of the assistant nurse managers thought I was stepping on their toes, doing so much. I told her I would welcome any help that anyone would be willing to give me. So I went around to all the assistant nurse managers and together we put the final touches on the workshop. They were a great bunch, and they chipped in to help. By Friday evening, we were ready to go with a Monday morning start up.

Monday morning came very quickly and I didn't even remember much about the weekend. I was so tired, I do know I spent a lot of it sleeping Sunday afternoon. But Monday morning I rolled out of bed at 4:30 a.m. and found myself walking into the old education and training department at 6:00 a.m., as I had done so many times before, setting up for a mandatory education day. It was almost deja vu, as I opened those doors and walked the empty halls. I thought back to my old manager and wondered what she was doing and felt sad that I hadn't seen or heard from her. I remembered our friendship and was sad that we hadn't kept in touch. The vendors and I set the food up, and made the final arrangements for the testing stations.

The morning was a blur, as we had so many nurses come through. The nurse managers, assistant nurse managers and my manager all came over, and we simply took the nurses through a mock set up of the competency testing for the day. I left a little bit early, as the day ended at 4:30 p.m., and by 5:00 p.m. I was out the door. The next morning I rolled out of bed feeling shaky, but I was at work by 6:30 a.m.. About 3:30 p.m. everybody had pretty much gone through. Everyone left.

A couple of people had signed up to help me tear down the stations, but by 5:00 p.m. nobody came so I began cleaning up by myself. Finally the nurse manager from the SICU department sent Rick, a nursing assistant, to help me move some of the heavy equipment I couldn't move myself. I put all the extra books in boxes, loaded up equipment on to carts, and he helped me push them over to the main hospital. It was almost 7:00 p.m. when I left. I went home feeling we had achieved a large accomplishment to get as many nurses through as we could. The books would now go to the individual departments, and the nurses could study and prepare on their own.

The week was going fast and on Thursday morning as I looked in a mirror I was very glad to have a hair appointment that night, my hair needed to be trimmed. I'd looked pale even though I had been out in the sun on several occasions. I couldn't seem to get my make-up color right. I didn't look well, appeared tired, and had deep, dark circles under my eyes. Maybe getting my hair done would make me feel better.

I went to the beauty shop to get my hair trimmed. I had an actual picture of what I wanted done. After I gave the beautician the picture I was busy talking, looking at the magazines and didn't pay a lot of attention to what she was doing. Suddenly I realized she had cut my hair too short. With the new perm, it kinked up even shorter, and I felt like Little Orphan Annie. It didn't style very well, and it looked worse. I left feeling uglier than I had going in. When I looked in the rearview mirror, I started crying. I was angry that I had not paid more attention. I cried all the way home. At one point I told myself I looked like a chemo patient and could actually see scalp through what little bit of hair I had left. When I got home I tried to straighten it by washing it. Melissa and Glenn were sweet and said it didn't look too bad and they assured me it would grow.

Just a little while later I heard a knock on the door, and it was my friend Kim. She had been my regular hair stylist for years. Kim commented that she knew I wasn't pleased with the way my hair looked, and also assured me it would grow. She offered to style it for me, but I had just washed it and it did look better. But, I hated my hair and I just shook. I really couldn't understand why I felt so angry. I knew I didn't look horrible and had to stop crying or my eyes would still be swollen in the morning. I had to teach an ACLS class the next morning, and couldn't have swollen eyes.

I went to bed early but when I awoke my eyes were swollen almost totally shut. Not to mention that my head hurt and I felt sick to my stomach. I didn't feel like teaching Advanced Cardiac Life Support but knew I didn't have a choice.

When I got on the elevator that morning, I saw one of the physicians that had always been likely to yell and scream, rant and rave at us. We knew each other well. We exchanged cordial 'good mornings', but he stared at me. I thought he was looking at my swollen eyes, and probably wondered what in the world I'd done to my hair.

I walked over to education and training classroom and started teaching. I had one physician, a young resident, who came into my therapeutic modalities testing station who didn't have what he needed. He had not studied, couldn't remember the algorithms, and the poor guy was paged two or three times in one algorithm. I finally told him, to go away and study for awhile, come back and try it again. And next time, leave his beeper with someone else. I didn't really feel comfortable passing him at that point.

Nancy, a good friend, came into the classroom after the resident. She was from Southwest Nine. She always had the most beautiful smile and was happy to have passed a lot of her stations already. She knew her stuff backwards and forwards and it was a pleasure to pass her. She made my whole morning. She was with another friend that we were both trying to help get through ACLS. She'd had a hard time, and was going through a divorce with a husband who had been pounding on her door, trying to get her to let him in half of the night. She really, really looked tired. She came in and couldn't remember one algorithm from the other. I felt sorry for her and my heart just went out to her. I sat and talked with her for a long time. Before I knew it, it was almost one o'clock in the afternoon. We finally agreed that she would do the testing next month, and that she would go and study some more. She just had too many personal problems to really deal with ACLS at this point in time.

I got up and helped Nancy put away the equipment from the ACLS class. I told her I was going to go home since I already had over forty hours that week, I was tired, and had another terrific headache.

CHAPTER NINE

The Diagnosis

When I got home, I knew why I felt so bad: I had one of my infamous bladder infections. I took some medicine and lay down. When Glenn got home I was asleep on the sofa. We ordered supper out but I spent most of the night on the sofa, sleeping off and on. The next morning I work up early, crawled out of bed quietly, about 8:00 a.m.. I called the hospital where my physician worked, and asked him to order me some medication. He was very nice about it and called in some medication to my local pharmacy. I went back to bed. Glenn got up about 9:00 a.m. to get to a deacon's meeting but I told him that I was going to stay in bed all day. He and Melissa could do whatever. He went on to his meeting and Melissa went to work. I had just dozed off to sleep when the phone rang.

As I reached over to pick up the phone, I literally smashed my left breast. It was Allen, one of the men from our church asking if I would continue to teach the Sunday School class. I told him I really didn't know and would have to pray about it but I would give him an answer next week.

When I hung up the phone I realized that I should probably check my breast. I checked the right one first and I didn't feel anything unusual. I reached over to my left one, and I felt this little hard knot, about the size of the end of my finger, making me feel kind of sick. I knew that I had never felt anything there before. I kept feeling around this area, then went back and felt it again. Sure enough it was real. It wasn't something I was imagining. It was real. It felt just like those little hard pea lumps that we had in those little artificial breasts that we carried around when teaching breast self exams to women. I had taught hundreds of women how to do breast self exams with those little fake breasts.

Now I was feeling one of those lumps right there in my own breast and it really gave me an odd feeling. I had fibrocystic breast disease, so my breasts were kind of lumpy anyway. But this was different and it felt different. As I lay there, a cold chill just went through my body. There are no words to describe it. It was as if I knew that this wasn't going to be a good thing. I tried to put those thoughts out of my mind, thinking only positive thoughts. But something wasn't right.

Glenn came home from his meeting and I had taken a little nap. I heard him downstairs, and I quickly reached up and checked my left breast again to see if I had maybe had a bad dream. But no, the reality was there. There was a small lump right on the gland in the 9:00 position of my left breast. Glenn came upstairs asked how I was feeling. He had gotten my medicine. I told him I had been drinking water all morning and felt a little better. I took my medicine and made small talk with him about the meeting. Finally I got up to take a shower and wash my hair. Once again I checked my breast, hoping maybe the lump had gone away.

My medicine began to ease the bladder discomfort and I went downstairs. I watered a few of my flowers while Glenn mowed the yard. It was hot, one of the hottest Julys we had had in a long time. It was a beautiful day, and I love hot weather, so it didn't really bother me.

I tried to do my Sunday School lesson but my heart really wasn't in it. I continued to work on it though and it wasn't too long before I got absorbed in the lesson. Every week I would try to make it more adaptable to the women in my class, so that we could take the lessons that we were learning and use them in our everyday lives. It gave me a feeling of satisfaction and peace to put the lesson together and I thought about what I had told Alan earlier that morning. So I sat at the kitchen table and prayed that the Lord would give me the words to speak, not just for that morning, but whether or not He would want me to teach this next year. Was I really being effective? Was I doing what He wanted me to do? I thought about the lump I had found, and asked the Lord to tell me where to go from here, and what to do. Oddly enough, I didn't feel unusually frightened or scared I somehow knew that the Lord would take care of it.

When Glenn came in from mowing, we went upstairs, and I finally had enough courage to tell him about the lump. He felt it, and said that we would need go get it checked. But I put it out of my mind. That evening my bladder infection was better and we went out to get a hamburger, looked around one of the malls, and watched some TV.

The next morning I taught my Sunday School class. We always start our class with prayer and I told my class that I had found this lump in my breast, and we went on with the lesson. We went out with friends of ours after church for breakfast and the day was an unusually quiet Sunday.

Monday morning I got up and called the doctor that I had been seeing and asked for an appointment. He could see me that afternoon so I went in and I asked him if he would check my breast. He said he didn't think it was anything at all to worry about. After all, eighty percent of all breast lumps are benign, and mine was in the 9:00 position of my left breast. He added that about three percent of those lumps were ever malignant, so he didn't think I had anything to worry about. But the little voice down inside of me disagreed and a little voice inside said, "No I think I want this one biopsied."

I tried to explain to him that this one felt so much like those little lumps in the fake breasts for self exam teaching, I didn't like the way it felt, and would feel better having it biopsied. He said he didn't think it was necessary, but if I wanted to do that, to go right ahead. I went out to his desk and I talked to his receptionist who said she would try to get me in to see one of the local surgeons. He couldn't see me for a couple of weeks and said I had to bring $50 cash as he wouldn't accept checks or credit cards, it had to be cash. I thought this was strange. I would just forget about this character and go somewhere else. The receptionist tried to get me in for a mammogram at the hospital since I was due for one in August anyway. However, they couldn't schedule me for a couple of weeks.

Nothing worked. I felt helpless and I had this feeling of urgency. I definitely had to have it checked now and didn't want to not know what was going on. So I went ahead and took the appointment for the mammogram but on the way home I decided I was not going to wait. I stopped by the hospital and canceled it. I realized I could go to the hospital where I worked and they would do the mammogram right away. When I got home I called my manager, and told her. I also shared with her my very uncomfortable feeling about this and the fact that I didn't think it would have a good outcome. My words even shocked me.

The next day I went to work as usual, and told Diane what had happened. She was very supportive and walked with me to the x-ray department. Of course our hospital scheduled my mammogram immediately and I had to wait only a few minutes before going in. I knew the technicians from my classes the year before. They were so nice, friendly. I can't say enough about their kindness that day. As I waited, one of the technicians came in and explained that since I had found a lump, the doctor wanted to come in and check me. I agreed that this was important and laid there waiting in the temporary examining room. The hospital was in the process of putting together a whole new breast center, but I had to wait in a storage room. There were gowns and all kinds of things stacked around. I felt terrible, as if I had been pushed into a closet.

However, through the closet door came this very young, handsome physician. He was very brisk in his approach to me. I tried to explain to him that I had found a lump, and showed him where it was. He kind of mashed around on my breast a bit roughly and said he didn't feel anything. Again I tried to explain he wasn't feeling quite in the right place, showing him where the lump was. He felt a little bit more and said, "I don't feel anything. I just think you're being a nervous nurse." And out the door he went.

For the first time I felt like I wanted to cry, I felt so exasperated. I reached up very timidly and felt the lump. I was sure it didn't get smashed away in the mammogram machine. But no, it was there, just this hard little round lump. It hadn't gone away and he hadn't really taken the time to examine me very well.

When the girls who had done the mammogram came in I shared this awful experience with them. He had said very confidently that he couldn't find it, but it is there. It's really there. I knew that I would need another doctor. Where do I go next? Who do I turn to? I don't know any of these doctors around here. Do I go back to my home town? Do I go here at work? I had a doctor a year ago, who did some minor surgery on my leg and I thought he might consider a biopsy on me. I called Dr. Jones' office right away, only to find out that he was on vacation and wouldn't be back for two weeks.

When his receptionist came back on the phone, she explained that someone was taking his calls and I could call him. I would explain I had found a lump in my breast, that I wanted it checked by someone relatively soon, preferably that day, and I would match my schedule to theirs. What luck, the doctor agreed to see me on his lunch time. I was very grateful and couldn't believe he was actually going to see me on his lunch time.

Glenn and I had driven to work together that day, because he wanted to provide as much support as possible. When he came to pick me up I told him how silly I felt since the results of my mammogram were normal and didn't show any lump at all. Glenn insisted we had come this far and would not stop now. The lump needed to be checked out. From the firmness and authority in his voice, I knew that there would be no getting around it, no going back now.

We walked in and told the nurse at the desk who I was, and she got up immediately and ran into the back. Another nurse came into the waiting room and showed me into an examining room, gave me a gown and said that the doctor would be in shortly. I had never met this man, I was nervous, and I felt shy. He came in, a short, little man, balding, probably in his mid-to-late thirties. He had a nice smile, and kind of a brisk manner about him, but I didn't want to focus on anything. He started the conversation with an abrupt, "You've got a lump, huh?" I thought to myself, this does sound familiar; it must be the standard way physicians greet women who have lumps. As he palpated my breast, he acknowledged that there was a small lump.

Again he went into the same long gyration about only about twenty percent of all breast lumps are malignant, and only three percent in the 9:00 position are malignant so he didn't think I had anything to worry about. He asked me all the routine questions, such as is there anyone in our family who has ever had breast cancer, or lumps, or anything like that? My mom had a lump that they had been watching for years, but it was nothing. It had never developed into anything. I hadn't had any injuries and was generally healthy. I did tell him I had had this severe fatigue, but he laughed and told me that all nurses are tired. But I did explain to him that I would just feel better if he would biopsy it.

He agreed to do a needle biopsy right then and pulled out a big, long needle. I watched as he put the syringe on it, and he came over and cleaned off my breast. I asked if he was going to numb me first but his response was that a needle stick was a needle stick and numbing wasn't necessary. Not reassuring!

I laid down, and he jabbed at the lump. The pain was excruciating and I didn't know if I could really stand it. The tears sort of sneaked out the corner of my eyes, and I tried not to cry, but I couldn't believe how badly it hurt. He spoke rather quietly when he commented that it was pretty hard, and not a cyst. He would try again. He jabbed again, and it hurt even more the second time. He pulled the needle out, and he went over to the cabinet and turned his back to me as he tried to get something out of the syringe to put on a slide. But there was nothing there, the syringe was totally empty. There was no kind of tissue.

I kind of laid there just feeling dazed and hurting, not quite realizing what had just happened to me. I had never had anybody treat me quite like that, without any kind of anesthesia. I thought about how tough it is for women that we have to go through this with lumps and wondered if all women have to do this. He sat me up, asked me if I was alright, and examined me again. He looked at the mammogram from last year, and compared the one from this year.

As we talked and he told me the story about a younger woman who had come to him. Nobody would listen to her, and she was in third stage breast cancer. That didn't make me feel a whole lot better, and I kept requesting the biopsy. As he walked towards me he patted me on the arm and agreed to do a biopsy just to put my mind at ease. He continued to pat me on the arm and asked me when I wanted it done. I said tomorrow will be fine. He laughed and said he couldn't get me scheduled by then. However, his nurse must have been standing outside the door, because she opened the door and she said they had a cancellation for the next morning at 8:00 a.m., and could certainly get me in for a biopsy in the morning.

Dr. Jones seemed pleased and wrote the prescriptions for the necessary pre-admission testing. It was set and I was to have my biopsy the next morning.

I didn't tell any one else at work, except for Diane and my manager. When I got home, Glenn and I told Melissa that I would be having a biopsy. Melissa assured me that it would be OK. We all sort of felt that way too. However, I denied this strange feeling deep down inside.

The next morning we got up early. I actually took some work with me to do while I was waiting to go into surgery, as I knew I would have about an hour wait in the pre-op room. I took a book on the implantable cardiac defibrillators to read and to bone up on so I would have all the information I would need to start an education program in our hospital. The nurses laughed as I waited to go into surgery, saying that nurses are always working, always doing something. I laughed with them.

It was a gorgeous, beautiful July day. I could see the sun from my cart by the window. The book I was reading did have some humorous places in it, the author talked about having an AICD implanted and how he laughed in the face of death. I enjoyed reading it, and I finished my project before I went to surgery. I had laughed with him and with the nurses and wasn't nervous at all.

I didn't feel particularly scared as they wheeled me into the surgery suite. I was glad to get the ordeal over with. I knew that I was getting "Versed." I wondered what it would be like. It is often called conscious sedation, because they say that you talk but remember absolutely nothing. The next thing I remembered clearly was Dr. Jones' voice telling me to wake up. He said he was sorry to tell me this, but my tumor was malignant.

I didn't know what to say and I just looked at him and said, "You wouldn't kid me about a thing like that, would you?"

The next thing I remember clearly was sitting in a chair, and Glenn sitting there beside me. He was so pale, and his face was so drawn, I couldn't believe it. I felt such a sadness for him. I really hadn't told anyone else, but Glenn had to sit through this whole thing and be told this awful news all by himself. No one was there to help him deal with it and I felt so bad, loving him so much. I remember holding his hand when Dr. Jones appeared from nowhere at the foot of the chair. He was talking to me, saying that he had removed the lump, but I would still need to make a decision about whether to have a complete mastectomy or a lumpectomy, whether I wanted radiation or chemotherapy. I slipped back into a sleepy somnolent state again.

I remember very little about the ride home, except Glenn holding my hand, and telling me that he loved me, and that none of this would make any difference to him. I slept most of the evening and woke up sometime around 6:00 p.m.. Glenn had told Melissa, and I knew I had to tell my family.

It was a Wednesday, and I called my sister and told her I had some bad news. It was very quiet on the other end of the phone and she said she would call Mom who was in Zanesville visiting my grandparents. Shawn wanted to call her but I said not to do that. We would get her up here, and let her know somehow. I was so tired I didn't really feel like dealing with it. Glenn and Melissa had called our pastor and some people at work with the news. So I knew the word was spreading very rapidly that I had a malignant tumor.

I slept off and on the sofa. The Versed had done a number on me, and I couldn't quite stay awake for any long period of time. But I felt as if I'd lost control.

The next thing I have clear memory of was my Mom coming in the kitchen door. I wondered how she had gotten back to Middletown so quickly. Shawn had called her friend, and they had brought her up, feeling that I should tell her myself. She sat down at the end of the sofa beside me, took my hand and asked what was wrong. I told her that I had found a lump in my left breast, had it biopsied, and that the biopsy was positive, it was a malignant tumor. I tried to tell her as straight-forward and as truthfully as I knew how. I wasn't crying or hysterical in anyway. Mom just sat there and held my hand. I remember saying to her very distinctly, that it wasn't on my agenda, that I hadn't planned to do it. But it had happened to me, and I would have to have surgery, probably a mastectomy. I had decisions to make about what kind of surgery to have and I would be going back to the doctor for more complete information. He would be giving me a complete pathology report on Friday. I felt like I was talking about someone else and this really wasn't happening to me. Even my voice sounded strange, like it was far away.

The next day I decided to get up and go into work. I knew I had to clear up some things there. I was going to have to have surgery the next week, and needed to make these decisions. I started telling people at work that I had a malignant lump in my left breast. I decided I wasn't going to keep it confidential, as I felt women needed to know that I had had a normal mammogram, and that some of the physicians felt that I should just wait six months, like my original hometown physician. I told them how the one in the x-ray department had acted. I explained I had to convince even the physician who had done the biopsy to do it, that I insisted on it.

Diane was incredibly supportive, going everywhere with me that day, helping me clear things up. I remember telling one of the Assistant Nurse Managers on one of the units and she looked at me and said, "Boy, what a bitch." I thought that was a real insensitive thing to say, but I guess that was her way of expressing how she felt about cancer. It hadn't yet dawned on me that I had cancer. The word seemed cold, far away, as if it belonged to someone else. I knew I had to make decisions. I had lots of tears at times, they seemed to come in droves and then they would dry up and not be there at all. I got through the day overall with very few tears, got a lot done at work, and told them that I wasn't going to be back until the ordeal was over. Most of the people were very supportive, and very shocked. Most thought of me as being very healthy, so it was hard for them to understand.

I began thinking what my agenda would be for the next few weeks and months. I wanted to know about the types of surgery there were and what were my alternatives. What was better, radiation or chemotherapy? The word chemotherapy was frightening, and I felt panic thinking about it. I have had allergies to medication most of my life and don't do well taking medicine. The therapy to me was the most frightening thing that I could imagine and it frightened me even more than the word cancer.

I had been an oncology protocol nurse back in 1982 and 1983 but realized a lot can happen in nine years. Maybe things are better. Will I lose my hair? Would I become so sick that I wouldn't be able to work? What was my future going to be like?

On Friday I got the final pathology report from Dr. Jones and told him that I wanted to get a second opinion. I wanted to talk to an oncologist. So I called one of our hometown female oncologists. I have the highest, utmost respect for her, as I had seen her at the hospital. I had seen her interactions with her patients and knew she had cured a very dear friend of mine. I called her office, only to find out that she was on vacation for two weeks. I really wanted to talk to an oncologist.

The receptionist told me there was a new oncologist in town, Dr. Malcolm, and he would be happy to speak to me. He came right on the phone, introduced himself, and talked to me. I told him what was happening, and his kindness was unbelievable. He told me to come over, bring my husband, and we would talk. So Glenn and I left to meet Dr. Malcolm.

When I saw him, he didn't look anything as I had imagined him to look. He was tall and young. I thought he seemed so kind, his voice was even kind. He sat us down and he spent over an hour talking to us about chemotherapy, about radiation. He examined me and explained that he would need to examine me more. He did a history and a physical. I told him about the fatigue that I had been experiencing for the last few months, that I had called it 'my bone-tiredness'. He told me that it was a symptom, one of the subtle symptoms of cancer. I was able to look at myself in the mirror and see the color changes I had thought were aging were really due to disease.

I remembered telling Glenn one time earlier in the summer that my color was like a cancer patient's color. Little did I know at that time that it was a true statement. My mind raced from one thing to another. The thought of having a mastectomy petrified me, it petrified Melissa, and Glenn just sat and told me he would support me no matter what. He would love me no matter what the surgery would be. Dr. Malcolm assured me I could get reconstructed six months after the chemotherapy but I wanted to have reconstruction right away.

Dr. Jones gave me the final diagnosis on Friday: intraductal malignant carcinoma of the left breast. I didn't really know what that meant and wanted to look it up, but was afraid. I knew what I needed to know, that I had cancer, and that was enough.

I went to work on Monday, and worked a few more hours, clearing up a few more things from my desk. I was to see Dr. Jones and have him look at my incision. We were going to decide exactly when the surgery would be. He examined me and told me to keep wearing my bra so the incision wouldn't look too bad. I wondered why that would matter. I asked him to explain to the surgery to me and he drew in the air the way the incision lines would be, telling me that this was my breast and they would remove it. He said it so matter-of-factly, as if he were saying, "Pass me the peas." I couldn't believe it and tried to explain to him that I felt very possessive about my breast, and that my daughter who was just twenty had a hard time accepting this. I didn't think I could get my feelings across to him, told him I was going to talk to another woman doctor in Cincinnati, and that I had tried to get hold of Dr. Mary, who was an oncologist. But before I could even tell him that I had talked to Dr. Malcolm, he made the statement that he felt that I was just a 'female chauvinist.'

Something about that statement just made me so angry that I couldn't even deal with it at the moment. I just looked at him and thought what an insensitive thing to say to someone who's just been diagnosed less than a week with cancer. I felt cold towards this man, and didn't want him cutting on my body. But yet, I didn't know what to do. I went home and told Glenn what he had said and just cried. I remembered the book 'First You Cry.' I had seen the movie with Mary Tyler Moore, and remembered the tears. I thought this was one time in my life I was allowed to cry, and I did. I felt so possessive of my body and realized I had to decide what kind of surgery I wanted.

Melissa wanted me to have a lumpectomy. Dr. Jones had said you sometimes scar with the radiation, and you can scar very badly, to the point that they can't do reconstruction. I thought of my sensitivity to the sun and sensitivity to medication, still wondering what to do. I decided that I would go with the simple mastectomy and called Dr. Jones. The surgery was scheduled for Thursday, August 8th, but I felt depressed and out of control.

I felt as if I had been on a roller coaster and hadn't been strapped in properly: I was being beaten up by the ride, and about to be thrown out, yet afraid to hold on. I didn't know one thing from the other thing. I couldn't eat. Everybody seemed so supportive, a lot of people by this time had heard, and had voiced their prayers and support for me. By Wednesday I didn't get dressed. I stayed in my robe and couldn't face the thought of going to surgery, but I wanted the cancer out of my body.

There was an older women at our church who was going to surgery the same day. The church and all our friends were geared up to pray for both of us. She had had a malformation in her brain that needed to be removed. She was having brain surgery, and I thought she was lucky because she had Glenn's surgeon. I didn't know much about this Dr. Jones that I was putting my life in his hands. I only knew that I didn't think I liked him any more, especially after he had called me a female chauvinist. Maybe he wouldn't leave enough skin for them to put in a prosthesis to do reconstruction down the road. I thought that wasn't not fair. He's a professional, and wouldn't do that to me. But these thoughts kept going through my mind and I felt so angry and confused. He said having reconstruction right away might mask the cancer's return and he didn't recommend a plastic surgeon.

I remember I had talked to Mona, a friend at work, who had been my age and gone through breast cancer. She had told me in our conversation at work that there was a doctor in Cincinnati, a plastic surgeon, that she would recommend. I thought if I spoke with a plastic surgeon, I might feel better and it would give me some hope for the future. All I had was a name, but I went over to the phone and started calling. And I got through! A lady answered the phone by the name of Bonnie. She was so sweet, and wanted me to speak with Debbie, their nurse. I waited just a few moments, and Debbie came on the phone. She introduced herself and said she understood I had just been diagnosed with breast cancer. I told Debbie that I wanted to know about reconstruction, as my mastectomy was scheduled for the next day. I had all these decisions to make, and I needed to know if I could have reconstruction right away. I had asked Dr. Jones, he said no, that it could cause the cancer to return, and I didn't want that.

Debbie assured me that was not true. She suggested that I hang up, since I was calling long distance, and she would call me back.. She sensed I needed to talk to someone, and commented that I wasn't ready to go to surgery yet. I gave her my phone number and waited impatiently for the phone to ring.

Before the phone rang, I started crying again. I tried to get some composure, but could hardly speak. When the call came, Debbie just took over, her voice so calming. She started telling me the different things that could be done and that, yes, I could have reconstruction right now with this surgery. That they have surgeries that they can do, what they call Rectus Abdominis flap or tunneling. They could do saline implants, they could do silicone. There were a host of choices out there, but yet I had only been told of two: simple mastectomy or lumpectomy. I expressed to her how lumpectomy frightened me, because I knew that some of the statistics show that there is a higher recurrence rate at the end of five years, although statistically there is no real difference. I also told her about being afraid of radiation and burns. She agreed that with certain people that is a problem, but that wouldn't mean it would be a problem for me.

I talked to Debbie for a long time, and she went through all the different types of surgery that I could have. I hung up more confused than ever. Melissa had gone to class, and it was just Glenn and I. I told him I wished I had another woman that I could just talk to for a few minutes, who could give me some answers. Should I go down and talk to Debbie as she had encouraged? Did I believe her when she said I wasn't really ready for surgery yet? It was almost as if the Lord had answered my prayer. I didn't even really realize I had prayed a prayer, but He knew I needed another woman.

The doorbell rang and I went to the door. I very seldom go to the door in my robe, but today I did. There stood my friend Liz. She looked almost sheepish as she stood in my entryway. She said she had no idea why she was here. She had been on her way to the church to do some work, and suddenly found herself at my doorstep.

I put my arms around her and just praised the Lord, because He knew I had needed another woman. He had sent Liz to my house at that very moment to sit and talk with me. I told Liz about my conversation with Debbie and what she had said. Should I call my surgery off? Should I go ahead and have the mastectomy? What would she do, if she were me? She said she would speak with them. I knew that I could trust Liz for being honest with me. I looked at Glenn and asked him what I should do and he again assured me of his love no matter what I decided.

Liz offered to call the people at church and tell them I wasn't having surgery and I was to call the family.

My Mom's response was to question the delay, as the cancer might spread. I assured her that it would not spread any more rapidly now. I would go to the doctor's office to find out more. When I called Dr. Kurtzman's office, they gave me an appointment for 1:00 p.m.. They also told me that I was doing this a little bit backwards, usually you go to see the oncological surgeon first. But this time I was going to see the plastic surgeon first.

The next day Glenn and I drove to Cincinnati for the first time. We found the office without any trouble, and walked in. Bonnie greeted me by name and ran over and gave me a big hug. She sat me down in a chair, looked me straight in the eye, and said, they were so glad I was there and they would help me make my decisions as to what was best for me.

I had hardly been seated in the chair when down the hall came Debbie. Again, she reached out her hands to me as she offered to go through all the things that I needed. She had saline implants, she had silicone implants, and had picture notebooks of hundreds of women who had gone through this and had different kinds of surgery done by Dr. Kurtzman. I couldn't believe how natural they looked, especially how good it looked to me, facing this devastating surgery. For the first time I felt hopeful. I kept asking her if this could be done at the same time as the mastectomy and she said yes. I kept asking if it would cause the cancer to come back, and she reassured me that was the old school of thought. I could have reconstruction and come out of surgery with a new breast.

After Debbie had shown me all the pictures and talked to me about the different kinds of reconstruction, I met Dr. Lawrence Kurtzman. He is a tall gentleman, very young, who had kind of reddish-brown hair and a full beard. He seemed shy at first, but his warmth and kindness was very evident in his voice and approach to me. He talked to me a long time about what kind of surgery I would choose. I told him I thought I would go with the free flap. They would just take a free flap of my rectus abdominis muscle, as I understood it, and fat out of my abdomen, and recreate a new breast. And this could be done at the same time as surgery.

Dr. Kurtzman concurred, I met all criteria, not overweight, was young and healthy, a non-smoker. That was a big factor, as if I had been a smoker, they couldn't do it right out of surgery. I would have had to wait. I told him that it was pretty much the surgery that I was leaning towards. He then very seriously sat down and advised that this was a big surgery, actually two major surgeries in one. I would have a big abdominal surgery across the abdomen where they would remove the flap. Plus I would have the mastectomy. I would have J-P tubes and I knew what a Jackson-Pratt tube was, one on the front of where the breast would be, sort of under the arm and then one on the back. And I would have two in my abdomen. I would, however, probably be able to go home with those tubes.

I told him I didn't want to go home with tubes and couldn't tolerate it. I wanted to stay in the hospital until the tubes were out, then I would be willing to go home. At that point I didn't even think of cost or insurance, or any of those things. I just wanted to figure out what kind of surgery I was going to have.

After my talk with Dr. Kurtzman, we went on to meet with a Dr. David Hymes, who was the surgical oncologist. He, too, was a young, dark-haired gentleman, very kind and prepared to spend time with us. He sat down and spent another hour and a half talking to us about chemotherapy, answering all of our questions about the surgery and how it would be done. As we left the hospital that day, our questions had been answered. We felt a sense of relief for the first time in over a week. We felt hopeful, and I had a sense that maybe my body could be put back together again.

I had not really dealt with the fact that I was feeling as if I was losing a lot of my femininity. I kept thinking of women who had gone through this before. I thought of

Betty Ford, Nancy Reagan, Ann Jillian, people who were in the spotlight. I wondered why they had never had reconstruction. I couldn't figure that out, when it seemed to be so readily available, and in different forms. I had never heard of flaps and trams, and all of these things till today. When I saw the work that was done, it was beautiful. These women had real looking breasts, with real looking nipples. It was totally amazing.

Glenn and I were so thankful we had waited. We knew that once again the Lord's timing was perfect. We just prayed together and thanked Him for, sending Liz to my door that day, who gave me the courage to stop surgery the next day. We thanked Him for sending these people like Debbie and Bonnie and Dr. Kurtzman and Dr. Hymes, who seemed to really care about the outcome of my surgery, not someone who just drew a few lines in the air and said we're going to take your breast off here, here, and here." They had compassion, and they cared about what was going to happen to me. They cared about how I was going to look at the end of all of this.

We knew when we left that I had made the decision to do the free tram flap. They told us to think about it and to call them back in the next couple of days. They would set the surgery up for me. We went back home, and I told Melissa, Mom, and Liz. Everybody just seemed to be so supportive. I called my friend Diane, I called my boss, and I told her what I had done. Everybody just seemed to understand and to agree with the decisions that I had made with the help of friends and with the help of the Lord.

CHAPTER TEN

The Surgery

I had completed the work I needed to do and knew that surgery was inevitable. I also knew that chemotherapy was the route that I would have to take when surgery was over. Now I had to deal with my feelings, and with Glenn's feelings. I remember going upstairs, changing my clothes, looking at my breasts, and thinking about how I would really look, and wandering what really lay ahead. A feeling of sadness washed over me from deep down inside. It was a feeling I couldn't describe any other way. I wasn't depressed, because I had hope for the future. But I felt possessive of my body and really didn't want to lose it, or even any part of it.

I was frightened by the surgery. I didn't know whether to tell the staff that I was a nurse, or to let them think I was just an ordinary woman. I was afraid that I might be treated differently if they knew that I was a nurse, especially a critical care clinical specialist.

I kept telling myself that it's OK to feel sad, it's OK to still cry. But feelings of fear and sadness continued to consume my thoughts. I knew I had to focus on some more positive thoughts in my life, but again I needed answers. I needed to talk to someone else. I called Debbie, back at Dr. Kurtzman's office. Again she went through the surgery, and I felt better. But I really was dealing with something other than just body image. I began to realize that the feelings were focused on the enemy, cancer.

This unwanted thing had invaded my body against my will and I was angry. I didn't want to have cancer and I didn't want to have to go through chemotherapy. I was mad. When I finally came to grips with the fact that I was mad, I knew I could fight it. I remember a few days before surgery I was fuming around the house, trying to put my life in order. I had put my projects in order at work as best I could, and now my home. I was angry that someone else would be doing my work. I trusted people and I knew I had their support, but still it was my projects, my home, my life that was being put on hold.

I looked around this house we had built, everything we had designed and put together for what we had thought was going to be a beautiful future. Now it held no real meaning. The Lord had really taught me that this is just a house in which we are to live. A beautiful home is not everything. I was anxious and began a cleaning frenzy. I cleaned and straightened the knife and fork drawer, the refrigerator, and cupboards that had never been organized since we moved in. I found myself engulfed in doing housework. I tried to keep focused on the work before me, but thoughts kept flooding my mind. It was a warm, sunny day and I went outside to walk and to look at the flowers.

Before I went outside I asked Melissa to vacuum as all she was doing was watching TV. She hates housework and I sometimes think her main goal in life is to be a TV movie critic. However, I don't think there's much demand in Ohio for movie critics. It got on my nerves that she was sitting there watching TV when I felt that there was so much to do before my surgery. Deep down she was trying to accept what was going on with her mother, and maybe being reminded of her father's illness. I didn't think about how she might be feeling. Melissa seemed to be in limbo and unmotivated about her futrue. It appeared as if she didn't want to deal with her feelings. But I didn't want to deal with them either.

At that moment I was angry with her. I became furious because she was sitting there watching TV and asked her again in a forceful voice to help me. She exploded in anger and told me it didn't matter what the house looked like. I should be doing some things that are fun and should be out. I tried to explain that I needed to work and fun things weren't fun for me. Right then I felt better doing work. She didn't understand and maybe I didn't understand it myself. I don't know, but I had this intense desire to put my house in order. Melissa continued to yell at me and I didn't want to be yelled at. I her to stop and couldn't she see I was hurting? Please don't yell, I was doing what I had to do. But she couldn't understand.

I felt very angry and sad. I ran outside and yelled at her that I didn't need to be talked to like that. What would she do if I died? What if they don't get all of the cancer? What would they do without me? You would have to do it all, I yelled back at her. I ran out into my backyard and the tears ran down, down into the green grass. I laid down in the grass and cried. I didn't care what the neighbors thought or what anybody thought. The ground seemed friendly, the earth smelled fresh and natural. Finally I began to feel renewed.

I realized that I was being watched through the family room door and I looked into Melissa's face. I could see that she too was hurting. She was young and had gone through a lot; she lost her best friend, and almost lost both parents. I went in and asked for a hug. She shrugged and gave me a half-hearted hug.

I got her by the shoulder I looked her straight in the face, reminding her that we had to support one other. I needed her and she needed me. I ordered her to give me a hug. My face was still wet with tears and I could see that she too had been crying. We were able to come together about some of our feelings. There were feelings that words just couldn't express, fear of death, fear of pain, fear of the unknown.

I went back outside and looked around. I saw that because of the hot weather some of my flowers had died and unconsciously began plucking out the dead ones that were still among the live ones. I picked at weeds and pulled them. Pretty soon I had a pile of dead flowers and dead weeds that were wilting there in the sun. I looked at the pile of dead flowers and weeds. It was then that I realized that that's what I had to do: I had to allow those cancer cells in my body to die and be plucked from my body. I would have surgery and chemotherapy, just like I had pulled up those weeds and dead flowers that were living there among the live ones. It was a symbolic ritual I had gone through and I didn't even realize it till I sat there looking at those weeds.

I could never quite turn off my mind. I could never quite forget that I had cancer, and I had to go through this. Surgery was over a week away, and I wondered how I would manage to keep my thoughts and my sanity until then. I thought about going back to work, but no, I needed this time at home, time to rest and put my thoughts together so I truly would be prepared for surgery.

They had told me what big surgery it would be. The healing time required would be lengthy. The thing that frightened me the most was truly being a patient. I had never really been a patient more than just a day or so in the hospital. Even with my kidney stones, I would go in, pass them and come back home. But I knew that this would be a little bit longer surgery. I would be in the hospital about a week. I wondered what it would be like. I didn't worry about the pain; I'd had pain before. Kidney stone pain is about the worst pain that you can think of. So I wasn't afraid of that, but I was afraid of being taken care of. I knew that I would not be allowed to wear clothes. I would have to wear hospital gowns. I would have tubes, and I had never had a tube before. I had taken out lots of Jackson-Pratt tubes in my time, but I had never had one. The thought of it made of nauseated.

All these thoughts would go through my head as I cleaned out kitchen drawers and cleaned out closets. I went over and over in my mind these next few days the way I would try to handle this. I knew that humor was a real important part of getting well and felt I had to think of something funny, but nothing seemed funny to me. Nothing. I tried to watch funny movies, but I couldn't seem to laugh. I couldn't figure out where my laughter had gone. I wanted to find something that would make me have a great big belly laugh, to excrete those endorphines that would help me with the healing and the pain. But nothing. I read and I searched, but nothing. I just felt very sad and I couldn't laugh.

The last night that Glenn and I made love, before I went to surgery, was very tender and sweet. My husband liked breasts. I had short, heavy legs, and was always glad I had nice breasts. I felt sad for him, because I wasn't the only one that was losing something in all of this. My husband was losing the wife that he had always known and loved. That made me sad as I put the sexy black nightgown over my breasts for the last time. Would I ever feel sexy again? How could I make love to this man that I love desperately? I didn't feel whole, I'll never feel whole again. I told myself these weren't the thoughts I should be thinking, yet they were the ones that were in my mind.

Glenn came in the bedroom, and was surprised to see me standing there. I smiled and told him that I had my 'Intimate' perfume on. He came over and he kissed me gently.

He led me to the bed and just sat there with his arm around me. He told me I didn't have to make love to him. I didn't have to do this, that he loved me no matter what. My breast wasn't what made me the person I was. It was the person inside that he loved and wanted to stay with the rest of his life. He didn't just love me because I had two breasts. I looked into his eyes and wanted desperately to make love to him. I can't describe it in words, a longing, a desire, a feeling of completeness that I needed at that moment. I put my arms around him, kissed him passionately, and pushed him backwards towards bed. It was always wonderful to make love to Glenn, and for a few brief moments my mind didn't think about anything else but loving this man I had loved for so long. He returned my love and I knew that he would be there to support me through this.

I knew the next morning would be a very emotional day. I had arranged for lots of people to be there with Glenn this time, so he wouldn't have to go through this by himself. My Pastor Nolan was on vacation so our new Assistant Pastor, Rev. Terry Little, was going to meet us at the hospital. My Mom, my sister and other people would be there. Melissa would come down later and I arranged for our youth pastor, Shawn Watson, who was just a year or so older than Melissa, to sit and pray with her. I felt so grateful for these people that I knew would be there for my family. I knew we were as prepared as we could be for that surgery.

There was kind of a numbness that came over me. I had gone through my mental checklist. Everything that I had wanted to do was done. I was as ready as I could be for the surgery. We had to get up at 4:00 a.m. and I had forgotten how dark it is at 4:00 a.m. in the morning. Mentally I told myself it wasn't darkness. There was a light at the end of this tunnel and I **will** get through this. Glenn looked at me and asked if I was talking to myself again. I was happy to tell him 'yes,' but this time I was talking positively. I smiled and reached for his hand.

When I got up that morning, I showered and washed my hair following the directions they gave me. I even styled my hair, and away we went.

It was a long drive to Cincinnati The roads were quiet. Not too many people were on the road on that Friday morning. We made small talk but I felt drained of tears and emotion. In a lot of ways, I felt relief. It would soon be over and I wouldn't have to think about it anymore. It would be over with.

We followed the signs to a small room. It was very nicely decorated, but there was no one at the receptionist desk, just a place to sign in. I signed in and wrote Glenn's name down as the person who was with me. Finally a nurse came in and told me to put on a gown and slippers. She gave me a paper hat for my hair. So there we sat, waiting.

After a while other patients began to arrive. I looked at them and I wondered what kind of surgeries they were having. I wondered if any of them had cancer. A lot of them were joking and conversing with their families. Glenn and I just sat and looked through old magazines and thought the least they could do is have some recent magazines.

I watched and began to realize that the nurse was a receptionist and transporter as well. She had a triple role. I then went to a place to wait for surgery. It was very large, and as we went in they announced, "Here's Susan Miller for her mastectomy and transflap." Her voice droned on. There were nurses scurrying about in scrubs. The scrubs looked so odd to me, because some of them were right side out and some of them were wrong side out. I couldn't figure out why.

A nurse came to usher me back to a room. She said her name over her shoulder, but I couldn't hear because of all the noise. It was a nice room that had hardwood floors and very modern equipment, including a TV. They put me in bed, and told me someone would be in to start an IV. They also said an anesthesiologist, my doctor, and the "plastics" would be in to see me. My husband and some family would be allowed to come in before I left for surgery.

I looked at the nurses and realized that none of them could look me in the face. They looked down, checked blood pressure, etc., but none ever looked me in the eye. Someone had told them I was a nurse. I wondered if they felt sad or if they identified with me because they knew I was a nurse.

I gave them the same information time after time. The more times I gave it, the more angry I became. Finally my nurse, the one I had started with that morning, said to me, "I know you've answered these questions already several times this morning, but I have to document them on the admission sheet." I looked at her and I said, "Yes, I understand that. I understand I have to tell this one more time." But what disturbed me most was that she still couldn't look me in the face, she couldn't make eye contact. I looked at her and realized she was probably only a few years younger than I was and maybe she was feeling scared too. I wanted to tell to her not to be scared, it would be OK. But I couldn't say those words, they wouldn't come out. I just answered the questions that she asked.

Pastor Little came in and prayed with me, it was a beautiful prayer, for the Lord to give strength and healing and I was grateful. The tears returned briefly during the prayer, but when it was over I felt stronger. Glenn and I were alone for a few minutes. I told the Lord to take care of my husband as I loved him very much.

It was interesting to see how people looked at you on the cart. Everybody was watching and staring at me in my funny little surgical cap. When I arrived in the surgical suite it was cold. The people were nice and got me some warm blankets and they felt wonderful.

They put me on the table. Everybody was scurrying about, doing their jobs. I watched them set up the trays and get the instruments out. I heard them ask for Dr. Kurtzman's instruments and Dr. Hymes' instruments. I just watched and found it to be interesting. I didn't feel sad but I was very clinical at that moment.

Pretty soon someone came by and they looked at my IV. They said, "Well, let's put you over here." They pulled my right arm out and I realized somebody was washing my right arm pit. I asked what they were doing that since the lump was not my right side. It was on my left. The person stopped abruptly. I couldn't see his face for the mask, but suddenly there were a few muffled words in the background.

They said, "Mrs. Miller, we have to switch you around here."

I said, "What do you mean?"

They said, "Well, we need you to get off the table. Can you do that?"

I said, "Well, yes, I can get off the table." They switched the whole table around and started washing my left arm pit. I felt strange and suddenly realized they were going to take off the wrong breast. I felt panicky, but thought, at least they were on the correct one now. They were washing my left arm pit. Maybe this isn't happening, maybe it's all just a bad dream."

The anesthesiologist came out at that point, and she said, "I'm going to put you to sleep now, Mrs. Miller. You won't remember anything. You'll just feel very relaxed and when you wake up you'll be in the recovery room and it'll be all over. Would you please count for me." I remember going ten, nine,...and that was it.

CHAPTER ELEVEN

The ICU

The next thing I remember was waking up and thinking the pain wasn't too terribly bad. My arm hurt an awful lot but that would be where they took the nodes out. My belly hurt pretty good too, but I didn't feel much in the breast area. It felt kind of numb and I didn't think too much about that. But my arm hurt, and every now and then it would sting clear up to my neck, and I couldn't figure out why. I realized that I couldn't talk, and my chest hurt. I realized that sound I had heard many times before was a ventilator and thought the person next to me must be on the ventilator. I hear a ventilator. Ouch, ouch, why was my arm hurting? Oh, my arm, my left arm hurt so badly. I went to pull on it and it was tied down. I thought I would reach over with my right hand and untie that because my arm was caught on the side rail. Then I realized that my right arm was tied down. I thought to call the nurse and tell her that my arm's are tied down. I'm awake now, I don't need to be tied down. I'm not going to pull anything out. But I **don't** want to be tied down like this. I hated that feeling. When I went to say something, all I could do was cough, this horrendous coughing. I realized I was on the ventilator. At that point I looked down and could see an endotrachael tube coming out of my mouth. I questioned in my mind why I was on the ventilator. What's happened? Where was I? I tried to turn my head around, and I could see I was in the recovery room, and there were people there.

One of the young plastic surgical residents was there, and he told me the surgery was over and I was in recovery room. But all I could think about was why was I on the ventilator? I heard him order another unit of blood and realized I must have bled. I wanted to tell him to take the tube out of my mouth and began to buck the ventilator like I had heard patients do many, many times. I couldn't stop it, it just was uncontrollable. It was like a pressure inside of my chest that I couldn't stop coughing, and tears ran down my face. I knew my face hurt so bad, and my hands. I raised my head up and I got a glimpse of my hand. I couldn't believe what I saw.

My hands were huge, my fingers weren't fitting together. They were hurting so badly, because they were so swollen. I didn't understand the awful edema. I looked around at my right hand, and it was swollen too. I thought I must be in terrible shape. I heard someone say to give me some Pavulon and at that point I got angry. I didn't want any Pavulon and shook my head, No, No, No.

They said, "Go ahead and give it to her; calm her down. We've got to get her calmed down, she's bucking the ventilator."

At that point the resident told me they had to take me back to surgery. I went into sort of a semi-slumber state. I could still hear people talking; I know they didn't know I could hear them, but I could. I heard the words they were saying. They were saying that I had bled, they were worried about the flap, worried that maybe it wasn't getting enough blood supply. Checking my flap, and looking at my new breast. I thought I want to see it too, but they raised my gown up in such a way that I couldn't see.

I tried to lick my lips, because all at once I felt like my lips were going to burst. I could feel that they were swollen, my tongue was swollen and my mouth was so dry. I would shake my head against the ET tube, and they would say, "No, give her a little bit more, give her a little bit more." Then I would sink into this well of nothingness. But I could still hear them. I thought, "They think they're so smart. They think I can't hear." I heard the nurses checking the blood, and hanging more blood. I heard them talking about my blood pressure.

Every now and then my left arm would sting and burn and I realized I had an arterial line in my arm. That was the Heparin burning my arm like that and couldn't understand why they kept irrigating the arterial line. No wonder I was bleeding. They didn't need to irrigate that arterial line so much. Look at how much Heparin is in that bag. If I could just focus a little bit more, I could read that. I have good distance vision and I knew I could read that bag. They thought I was out of it, but I wasn't. I was watching them, could see them scurrying about.

What were these things on my legs? Oh, those were those compression devices, those automatic compression devices. They were so hot and sticky and I would like to have those things taken off my legs. I want an ice chip, just one ice chip.

I also wanted somebody take a cool cloth and run it across my head, somebody to give me something to clean my mouth. I had this awful ET tube, my mouth felt terrible.

What time was it? But nobody would tell me what time it was. I drifted in and out of my semi-conscious state for awhile. I had no sense of time, only a sense of time passing. I didn't know if I had gone back to surgery yet, or not. I felt tired, I didn't feel like I could fight anymore. I didn't feel like I could turn my head anymore. I wanted to get the ET tube out, I wanted the compression devices off my legs, and I wanted to be untied. It felt like hours, maybe days. I wondered if it was still Friday. I didn't know, nobody told me anything. People came and looked at my flap, and said it still looked pink, and away they went.

I had a sense of being all alone, there was nobody around. I felt frightened, and wanted somebody with me. I didn't want to be alone. Nurse, where was my nurse? Nurse! I shook my head side to side. She came and I mouthed the word 'ice, ice'.

She said she couldn't give me ice, it would make me throw up and I had to go back to surgery. I would throw up if she give me ice.

I realized I wouldn't throw up. My mouth, those mucous membranes were so dry, little tiny ice chips would be absorbed. It would never get to my stomach. Didn't she know that? Just one little ice chip to moisten my lips and my tongue as they were cracking. I could feel my lips crack every time I would move my mouth even just a little bit. The slits in the corners of my mouth became sore and open.

I realized I couldn't open my eyes like I had before. I looked out and could see that my eyelids were swollen out over my eyelashes. I could actually see the fluid and the tissues in my eyelid. I felt stinging in the corners of my eyes as water began to run down my face and thought it amazing they couldn't see what was happening to me. I desperately needed some kind of skin care. My wrists hurt from being tied down, and I'd been tied down for a long time. But she just looked at me and said, "You're going back to surgery," gruffly.

I wondered if she would treat a dog like this? I wanted her to explain to me, talk to me, tell me why she couldn't give me mouth care, why she didn't put a cloth on my eyes. I had done it for my patients and took good care of them. One little ice chip wasn't going to cause vomiting. It would cool the tongue, decrease the swelling, and make my mouth feel better. Cream on the lips helps them to keep from cracking. Vaseline on the eyelids keeps them from cracking. I desperately wanted someone to give me some nursing care. I had done it for years and wanted someone to take care of me. To release my restraints for just a moment and let my fingers come back to life, they felt so dead.

I cried inside and just couldn't believe I couldn't have nursing care. I wanted someone to take care of me like I had taken care of all of the countless patients I had. But there was no one there. When I looked around the room, there was no one, they were all gone. I drifted off into sleep, and I didn't remember anything for a long time.

The next thing I remember was hearing a nurse asking the doctor about PVCs, premature ventricular contractions, an irregular heart beat. She said something about she was having a lot of PVCs. I thought I always had PVCs, don't worry about PVCs with me. I heard the doctor say to wait awhile before they did anything else and to give me another unit of blood.

I don't know what time it was, because I slept again. I had no time frame, no thoughts, no nothing. The next time I awoke it seemed to be a little more peaceful. I looked around the room and there wasn't anyone there. It was totally empty, there were no other patients there, no nurses, no physicians. I looked up and I could see that I was no longer attached to the ventilator, but still had the ET tube in place, and it was hooked up to a nebulizer.

I felt strange, more swollen than I had before. My fingers felt like they would never go together again. My mind seemed a lot sharper, clearer than it had before, but I was still frightened and wanted someone to be with me. And yet as I looked and peered around that recovery room, there was no one there. I thought to myself it had to be

Saturday by now and on Saturday they didn't have as many surgeries. I must be in the recovery room on Saturday. But why wasn't someone here to take care of me. I knew what I would do with my legs free. I had the compression devices on my legs, but I would kick one of them off and it will make a noise, and somebody would come. I bent my knee and was pleased it still worked. I began to kick and squirm, and sure enough, pretty soon I got it off, and it crashed to the floor.

A nurse came running, a tall blonde and I remembered seeing her face before. She was nice, grabbed my hand, and held it saying, "We'll see about getting that ET tube out now." I thought that was wonderful, couldn't wait, but yet I wondered what that was going to feel like. I didn't know what it would be like to be suctioned. Pretty soon they were at the top of my head, and said, "We're going to suction you out now, Mrs. Miller." As they suctioned me out the pressure inside my chest was unreal. I realized this was what it felt like to my patients when I suctioned them. It was so uncomfortable, as I gagged and heaved into the ET tube.

"That's enough. I'll go down one more time and the next time we'll pull it out." I saw her release the air from the catheter. The anticipation was awful and then it was coming out. What relief to get that out of my chest and out of my throat. It was a sense of relief and I felt like I could go to sleep now and sleep forever.

I realized that my arm hurt, and my new breast hurt. It was the first time I had really thought about it for awhile and wondered what it looked like. I strained, but I couldn't get my head up enough to see. But I had one accomplishment and had the tube out. And I drifted off back to sleep.

I don't know how long it was before I woke up again, but they were telling me they were going to take me to my room. I realized I could talk now and wondered where Glenn, Melissa, Mom, everybody else was The nurse assured me that my family would be right in. She would let them walk down the hall and they could go up to the ICU burn unit. That surprised me and I asked why I was going to the burn unit.

The nurse said that it was because we take care of flaps there and that was where all the experts were who knew all about that flap I had. That explanation helped me understand the reason for the move.

I turned around and saw Glenn's face. I was thrilled and didn't know if there were other people there, it seemed as if there were, but I couldn't really see them. I saw Glenn and he told me it was all over and reached for my hand.

I felt so strange, not at all like me. I felt huge, so swollen and wondered what had gone wrong. I raised my hand up and looked at it. It was unbelievably swollen, beyond my wildest imagination. I had seen patients' hands look like that and said out loud, "I've third spaced fluid that is stored in the tissues." Glenn looked at me and asked me to repeat what I had just said. I repeated, "I've third spaced all my fluid. I'm all swollen up. I must look like a real sight to you."

He said, "No, you look like my Missy, and I'm glad you're coming out of there."

They put me in a private room in the burn treatment ICU. They explained that my PCA pump would allow me to administer my own pain medication through the IV line by pushing a little button. When they moved me from the cart to the bed, the pain became very real. It was pretty bad, but yet it really wasn't as bad as I imagined it to be. I didn't really hurt quite as bad as I thought. My arm hurt the worst, it just felt a tingly, sharp, spiny like pain almost all the time. I looked and realized it was an arterial line. That was what was wrong with my arm. It looked different than any arterial lines I had ever seen where I worked before. They had a whole, totally different set up and I tried to figure out how they calibrated it. I couldn't help but think how they do things a lot different here than what I had done in the past.

It felt so good to be in bed and Glenn was permitted to stay for a few minutes. I asked for the PCA pump to get some drugs for the pain. Glenn asked if I was tired and told me that my Mom and Miss were there. I was tired but did want to see them. My Mom brought me the prettiest white kitten, it was all white fur. She laid it there on my pillow. She said she thought I might feel lonely, and I would feel better if I had the cat with me. It was just so good to see her face. Miss was there, and she brought me a rose, and a little bunny. I remember the rose, because they attached it to the window and I could see it every time I turned my head.

They didn't stay very long, the nurse literally pushing them out, saying only two visitors are allowed. This gruff voice came out of nowhere, out of this little tiny woman. I couldn't help but think that here was another nurse who sounded so mean. Why did she sound so mean? Had I been so bad? Am I such a terrible patient that she has to sound that way? Her voice seemed to fill the room. She told them she was going to take my blood pressure. She whipped up my left arm, and I pleaded with her not to take my blood pressure in my left arm and reminded her I had a mastectomy and to take it in my right arm. She agreed but not until after she actually admitted that she had forgotten.

But how could she forget? That's why I was here. I had a mastectomy and had cancer. But my cancer was gone now.

I watched her as she walked around the edge of the bed to take my blood pressure. She put a thermometer in my mouth, did her assessment, and made me take deep breaths, checking my dressing.

It was then I realized I had all these tubes. There were four of them and it felt like the whole bed was full of Jackson-Partt drains. They were full to capacity with bloody drainage. When I asked what happened, she mumbled something about me having had a bleeder. She got little paper cups and started measuring. Every one of them had 100, 150,

200, 250, I couldn't see but I watched her add, almost 400 cc in total drainage. I thought I was getting rid of some of that fluid. I realized I also had a Foley catheter. It felt kind of strange, but not painful, more like a pressure.

I kept trying to keep my breasts covered up. It seemed like everyone who came in uncovered me. I tried to reach up with my IV arm. I didn't have much use of those fingers, they were so swollen. I was glad I didn't have them tape my rings because with the swelling, they would have had to cut them off. I was very glad Glenn had taken my rings home.

I pushed the little button for a little bit more of what I called my 'joy juice', then drifted in and out of sleep.

It seemed like some time during the night I heard a burn patient start screaming at the top of his lungs. I knew it was a burn room, so I figured he must be getting his dressings changed. He was yelling, and I heard them say he was young. I felt bad for him.

My night nurse came in and she seemed nice but she, too, grabbed my left arm to take my blood pressure. I said again please, take my blood pressure in my right arm, I've had a mastectomy on that side.

Her response was, "Oh, yeah."

I tried to make some conversation as I was feeling a little more clear headed. I talked to her about how many patients they had and she immediately started into a long tirade of how short staffed they were, not enough staff, and she had umpteen burn dressings to do. It seemed like her voice just droned on and on. I was painfully reminded that I should not have asked, I wouldn't do that again.

She came with the cups, and she too drained almost full capacity out of the Jackson-Pratts. And she emptied what she said was over 800 cc of urine. I was glad to be getting rid of some of the fluid, that would make me feel better and I would be able to use my hands. I couldn't bend my fingers at all and it seemed weird to look at them so swollen. I also had a funny yellow tinge, which I didn't quite understand, but thought maybe it was because I still had a lot of the betadine antiseptic on my skin.

Then I pushed my little button, and I went off to sleep.

I don't know what time it was I woke up, but I was uncomfortable. I kept thinking I smell like a patient. It hit me like a ton of bricks: that's what I did smell; it was me. This bloody, foul smell was me. It floored me. I was in an Intensive Care Unit with an arterial line, IVs, Foleys, and 24-hour nursing care. But where was my nursing care? I reached down and felt something wet on the bed. I thought I had wet the bed, but I couldn't have done that, with a Foley in. Did I have diarrhea? I raised my hand up, and my hand was covered with bloody drainage. I realized one of my Jackson-Pratts had opened and it had drained in the bed. It was then that I became aware that there was this bloody fluid dripping between my legs.

I had two Jackson-Pratts draining at the top of my left breast, and two in my lower abdomen. I was draining almost a continuous stream down over my whole lower body, all over my pubic area. My bed was full of fluid. I put my light on and waited and waited and waited. After a long time the nurse arrived and asked what could she do for me? I told her about the mess in the bed and how awful I felt, I wanted to be cleaned up.

She said, "I'm sorry, I don't have time right now. I'm in the middle of doing burn dressings." Here, roll over. Let me put some of these chux in bed with you."

She put these plastic chux right next to me and I thought I had never put chux next to my patients' skin. They immediately stuck to me, like some kind of glue and actually made me feel worse than I did before. I knew I wanted to be cleaned up, but the nurse was gone out the door. I was sure that I would get a bed sore laying in this mess. I tried to move, but seemed glued to the sheets. The smell was atrocious, and it made me nauseated. I realized I couldn't get out of the mess right now and she wasn't going to get me out of it either.

I could hear the patient screaming at the top of his lungs and in spite of my own misery, felt bad for her. I thought there had to be other nurses here. Why weren't they around to take care of patients? Only one nurse? But I decided I would just give myself a little more of my Demerol. I pushed the PCA pump, waited a few more minutes, and pushed it again. It was the first time I had pushed it two times in a row and I didn't know what dose I was getting. It didn't really matter as long as it made me go to sleep so I could forget. At that point I just wanted to go to sleep and forget about that awful, sticky, foul-smelling mess I found myself in. I looked at the clock as I drifted off to sleep. It was 2:15 in the morning.

The next time I woke up it was 4:15 a.m.. Two hours I had slept and I was still laying on those chux. I felt worse, and smelled worse than I had before. So once again I took the risk of putting my light on and seeing if I could get the nurse to clean me up. She came in, and she was in a little bit better mood.

She said she was real busy and they had such a terrible night, without help.

She started bringing in clean linens and folding things. I could tell she was a little bit upset, that she really didn't want to be cleaning me up. I couldn't say that I blamed her, but I really didn't make this mess because I wanted to.

She angrily flipped off the sheets, not realizing that my Foley was still attached to the sheet. The foley pulled I could feel the bulb in my urethra. It was ready to pop out. I Let her know she was pulling my Foley. Tears came down my face, it hurt so bad, an excruciating pain. The top of my head even hurt. I felt sweat come across my brow and I felt breathless from the pain. She looked sheepish and apologized, "Oh, I'm sorry, I didn't know that it was attached to the sheet." Then she shoved it between my legs, back up into the bladder. I thought that was just great, now I would a bladder infection on top of everything else. Now I have drainage on the Foley, and drainage inside of me. I felt panicky, and I just wanted to jump out the big window next to my bed. I wanted out of there and away from this woman.

She whipped off the covers and there I lay with nothing on. I dared to venture looking down at my new breast, but all I could see was a dressing. I was a little relieved, I wasn't ready to see it in this way. I lay there with nothing on, laying on the sheet, over on my side. The curtain was only halfway pulled, and other people were going scruffling about in the hall. I didn't have anything to cover up with, it was as if nobody cared, my modesty was removed along with my breast. It didn't seem to matter to anyone. She cleaned up my bed and wiped at my back and my rear and between my legs.

My mind raced. I knew I needed to be washed, needed to be cleaned up, and needed a bath. I wanted to tell her she could give me a bath now, and be done with me for the rest of the day, but I didn't have the courage to say anything. I felt afraid of this woman. She certainly wasn't a peer and she was far from friendly. She seemed irritated and angry, overworked and stressed. I had seen that look on nurses faces before. The more I thought about it, the madder I became. Why were they doing this to nurses? Why couldn't we have enough nurses to give the kind of care that this woman probably wanted to give, but couldn't, feeling the pressure of time.

I wondered if she didn't want to be a nurse that she was one of those nurses who became a nurse for some reason other than wanting to take care of the sick. I didn't know why but I knew I wanted someone to care and take care of me. It was my turn to be on the receiving end. Why couldn't someone give me good nursing care?

It felt much better, just to have clean sheets. I rolled over and again gave myself more Demerol, knowing that things would have to be better in the morning.

When I awoke, there was a line of men standing on each side of my bed. I realized that they were the surgical and plastic residents. They pulled all of the covers off of me. I glanced over to see if the curtains to the hall were pulled, and it had been, halfway. You could still see me laying there from the hall and I felt uncomfortable, like some kind of a specimen as they conversed over the top of me. Finally one of them addressed me and I was shocked he said something to me. I didn't really know quite how to respond. Gruffly he said, "Mrs. Miller! Are you awake?"

I responded immediately, "Oh, yes, I'm awake."

"Well, are you?" he asked.

"Am I what?"

"Are you having a lot of pain?" he quizzed.

I told him it wasn't too bad. I would take my Demerol every now and then, when I felt like I needed it. But it took care of the pain just fine.

He asked if I thought I might be able to get up today, and I said I would certainly try.

Then I heard them talking about my edema. I looked at my hands, thought with so much output, my hands, should have gone down, but they were still so edematous I couldn't begin to get my fingers together. It suddenly dawned on me to check my face. I reached up and touched it and I could tell that it was as edematous as the rest of me. My eyes had little tiny sores in the corner and little scabs were beginning to form.

I thought that was a good sign, but it would be nice if somebody would just let me brush my teeth, clean my mouth, but nobody offered. I looked around as the residents left as abruptly as they came, without a comment or anything, until they got halfway out the door, and said, "If you need anything, give us a call." I covered myself back up because they left me half exposed.

The next thing I knew a strange person was coming in and bringing me breakfast. Food did seem good and I thought I could eat a bite. I was raised up in the bed, but it suddenly dawned on me that I couldn't open any of the packages. My hands were too swollen. The art line and the IV in my hand restricted what little movement I did have. I was trying to be very careful, but I couldn't pour the hot water for coffee, and couldn't get the plastic off the containers that held the eggs, cereal, and milk. I finally put my light on to see if I could get someone to come and help, but no one came.

I managed to eat a few bites of the toast and pushed the tray away. Sometime later someone came in and asked what I needed. I told them I had originally wanted my breakfast tray opened up, that everything was either wrapped in plastic or professionally wrapped and I couldn't open it.

She offered to open the eggs for me and get the cereal ready but I said no, it was OK. By then I really didn't feel like eating cold eggs and cold cereal. I would wait and try lunch. I started to tell her that I couldn't do anything because my hands were so swollen, I couldn't bend my fingers, they didn't go together. She was out the door before I even had a chance to tell her why I didn't open it myself. I gave myself a few more bursts of my Demerol and escaped.

It was sometime later and I heard a nice voice telling me she was going to give me a bath. Oh that sounded wonderful, and were the most wonderful words I had heard in the two days I had been there. I never thought I would welcome someone giving me a bath, but I was overwhelmed with the sense of wanting to be clean.

After it was over, she pulled the curtain and she said to me, "Let me show you, I had a tummy-tuck four months ago. Let me show you how flat your tummy will be when this is all over." So she showed me her tummy. I was amazed at how flat and smooth it looked, but I explained to her I didn't do this just to get a flat tummy, I did it to get a new breast. I felt that I had never had a problem, my tummy had always been flat. We laughed and she told me how after three children, hers didn't even know the meaning of the word 'flat'. We talked about a lot of different things, about how long she had been there and how much she liked working in the burn unit. She really was very much a comfort to me that day, just to talk to me about sort of nonsensical things. I appreciated her so very much. She left after awhile, and I gave myself a few more Demerol spritz, and slept.

They brought my lunch, and it was pretty much the same story as breakfast had been. They brought it in and nobody offered to open anything up. I managed to open a small hole in the plastic wrap on the plate and eat some of the chicken.

It seemed that everybody moved so fast but I was groggy, and couldn't seem to communicate with anybody. They popped in and out, and I didn't always understand what they were doing or what was happening. I felt kind of foolish and thought I should be able to do some of this for myself.

In the afternoon the head resident of the plastic surgery division came back in. He asked me if I had been up, and I had told him that I was supposed to get up sometime that afternoon, but I hadn't yet. I asked him if I could get rid of the Foley and told him I'd feel a lot better if they'd take that out. He said I would have to go to the bathroom. I assured him I would get there , somehow. Just take that catheter out. He agreed. I also talked to him about taking the arterial line out, but he said he wanted to wait till morning and leave it in one more day. So I conceded, at least I would get rid of the catheter.

In a little while, my nurse came back in and said, "Guess what? We get to take the Foley out." I said, "I know." I was thrilled. It was wonderful not to feel so tethered to that bed. She told me to call when I felt like I had to to the bathroom for the first time. I assured her that I would. In the meantime I gave myself a little Demerol, because I was hurting.

I felt numb from my shoulder to my elbow, but yet that same stinging, burning pain just didn't ever seem to quite go away. It was like my arm had been electrified, with current flowing up and down from my shoulder to my elbow. I'd sort of gotten used to it, but the more I woke up, the more I became aware that it never really did stop. The rest of my pain was like a dull, aching type of pain, deep inside, but this was an electrical nerve-type pain that was hard to describe and difficult to endure.

In a little while the nurse came back in and asked if I felt like getting up. I agreed to try anything once and actually felt good about trying to get up. She rolled the bed up in almost a 'V' position. I said to let me do the rest. I pulled myself to the edge but didn't realize how bad I did hurt. When I stood on my feet for the first time, I felt my head swirl.

I said to myself, don't pass out, Sue, don't pass out. The room seemed to swirl, but I continued talking to myself. I knew I could control this and not pass out. I took a slow deep breath knowing that would increase my oxygen. I couldn't stand up straight; I was bent over. I told the nurse he must have taken about four inches out of my belly. She laughed and advised it would be like this for several days and you think you'll never be in an upright position again. It was nice talking to someone who already knew what I was experiencing, like somebody had put a spring in my belly, and I couldn't stand up. I was trying, but I'd spring back down.

We managed to make it to the chair, and I sat there for a while. It felt good and I watched the nurses out in the hall, scurrying around. I hadn't been up very long when suddenly I realized I had to go to the bathroom. My call light was lying on the bed, and I couldn't reach it. I tried and tried, but with those fat fingers I couldn't really get to that cord. I worked and I worked and I worked, and I still couldn't reach that cord. So I started to yell, "Nurse, nurse" every time I'd see someone go by. They'd all tell me, "Just a minute, just a minute." I kept thinking, "Gee, I hope I have a minute. I don't know how long I can hold this."

Pretty soon she came in and asked if I needed something. I said yes, I had to go to the bathroom. Suddenly she pulled a curtain that was in the corner of the room, and there was the toilet. I was very glad I didn't have to go very far. We grabbed the art line and the IV and my four little drain tubes, and hobbled me over to the toilet. It was horrible. How many times I had walked patients like this and had no idea how humiliating it was to be this helpless, having this utter, complete feeling of helplessness. I just felt engulfed in it and wanted to cry because I couldn't do anything for myself.

I sat my fanny upon the toilet and thought, "Oh dear, I wonder if I'll have trouble going after a Foley." But, no, I went and I went and I went and I went, and I thought, "Where did all this fluid come from?" I looked at my fingers and my hands and saw how swollen they still were, and I knew where it was coming from. I went to clean myself and suddenly realized that I couldn't bend my fingers to even wrap them around the toilet paper. My nurse came in and looked at me, and I felt embarrassed. She asked me what was wrong and I told her I couldn't even wipe myself. I couldn't move either arm, or bend my finger. I started to cry.

She put her arm around me and said, "Now you're a nurse. You know that we don' mind doing these things." I told her I hoped not, but I've never had it done for me before. I've never had to have anybody do this. I felt so helpless, so mortified by the whole experience. I just sobbed into her shoulder. She patted me, and was very nice. Very discreetly she wiped me and said it was payback time, for all those times I had done it for other people. I thanked her, but I really didn't want this payback. I wanted to be able to do things for myself again and I did my slow shuffle back to the bedside.

The pain was pretty bad by the time I got to the bed, and I could feel the beads of sweat on the sides of my face. She asked if I was hurting and I had to admit I hurt pretty badly. She urged me to use the Demerol. I was allowed to have it as needed.

I told her I was trying to get by with as little as I could with the hope I could get transferred to the floor a little sooner. She told me not to be a martyr about this, and gave me a spritz. I could feel the medication take hold and the pain subside, as I eased back and down into my pillow.

She had been the first nurse who had actually used some pillows to position my shoulders and back, so I wasn't always lying on my back. I told her how much I appreciated it, because I hadn't thought about how much time I had spent to this point on my back.

She told me I needed to be turned every two or three hours at most, because I really couldn't turn myself. I couldn't use those hands yet and wondered if I would ever get my hands down.

She assured me it would happen but was going to take a few days. I had really third spaced everything, and out the door she went.

I drifted off into a sound sleep and I didn't remember anything, until suddenly I was aware that Glenn was standing next to me. I asked him how long he had been standing there.

He said, "Not very long. I was just watching you sleep."

My Mom was at the foot of the bed, with Melissa kind of hiding in the corner. We knew why she was hiding, otherwise someone would come and run her out.

In a few moments, Liz and Bruce came, and Kim and Rob, and they all visited a couple at a time. I could see that Liz looked at me really strangely, and knew that I must look terrible. I was sure my face was still very swollen, if it looked anything like my hands. Suddenly the thought came to me and I wanted to see my face, to see what I looked like. Everybody had a paniced look on their face, and said, no, you don't want to do that. I insisted. I did want to see what I looked like third spaced. I tried to make my voice sound almost jovial in an impish way. Glenn looked at me with one of his sly looks and I pleaded, promising not to panic. I've already gone through the hard stuff, and it would be downhill from here. Glenn just slowly went over to the night stand, pulled the mirror and held it up to my face. I was totally astonished at how I looked. I was very swollen, my eyelids totally swollen out over my eyelashes. You couldn't see them at all. My lips looked like great big rows of bananas or something, they stuck out so far from my face. My hair was just sitting on top of my head with the rest of this big face hanging below my brown hair. My face had a yellow tinge, and I looked truly the clinical picture of third spacing.

89

I didn't know what to say. All these eyes seemed to be peering at me, waiting for my response. I looked at them and commented on no wrinkles. Everyone laughed. Silently I hoped when it went down it didn't leave too many wrinkles. If Dr. Kurtzman was as good as everybody says he was, he could just fix the wrinkles too.

We had a nice visit but Dr. Kurtzman came in and wanted to check me out in the midst of it. I heard Bruce and Dr. Kurtzman in the hall talking. Bruce being a doctor, I figured he would want to know everything that there was to know about the surgery. They didn't stay long.

Soon after, my sister and Will came in. I remember my sister looking at me real sheepishly. The nurse had come in to work on my arterial line and to empty my Jackson-Pratt drains. Shawn seemed engrossed in what the nurse was doing. I watched her eyes and thought maybe it was kind of hard for her to see her sister in this kind of shape in an Intensive Care Unit. After all, she was young and this was probably tough on her" She looked at me and said, "Sis, I've got to go, I've got to take care of the kids." I could tell something was wrong by the look on her face. I didn't know what it was and didn't really want to ask. I guess I didn't want to know the answer. It wasn't unitl a month later that she discussed with me the poor nursing technique she had observed that caused her negative reaction.

Glenn stayed and helped me eat my supper until visiting time was almost over. Right before the time was over, my neighbor, Bobbie Sitch, came in. She'd snuck in some pretty flowers. They were an unusual arrangement of daylilies and some kind of grasses and ferns, and it was beautiful. The nurse agreed I could see it, but she had to take it back. We weren't allowed to have flowers on that unit. She handed it to Glenn and he took it back with him when he left that evening.

I felt tired after all my visitors, but yet didn't want to go to sleep. I put the television on, but that didn't last very long. The next thing I knew the 3-11 nurse was emptying my drains and I told her I had to go to the bathroom, so she helped me there. This was a new nurse, one I had never seen before, and I tried desperately to remember her name, but I couldn't. I began to think there was some kind of mental block that I couldn't remember my nurses' names. She was pretty nice, took her time and helped me get to the bathroom. I walked so slow, and so bent over, I felt like I was ninety years old. But she complemented me and said I was doing pretty well for just my third time up. I was proud I had done that well. She straightened my bed, and I crawled back in and gave myself a little spritz of Demerol. I told her to turn the light out, I was going to try to sleep. She said she'd be back in before the end of her shift.

I slept fairly well that night. I would wake up and be hurting, that terrible electrical pain in my arm seemed like it would never go away. It sapped what little bit of strength I could muster.

A couple of times during the night I got up and slowly strolled to the toilet. It seemed like the fluid was just coming off in droves now. I had really hoped that my fingers would come a little more together and I could grasp my hands around a piece of toilet paper, but I just couldn't seem to do it. The arterial line and the IV were still in the way, even if I could have put my fingers together. I'd almost gotten used to the nurses wiping me but still felt humiliated and helpless. It was such a relief to climb back into bed after my little trek to the toilet that I really didn't seem to care.

The next morning I woke early with someone yelling and I wondered if everyone thought I was deaf. I looked into the face of the young residents of plastic surgery as they stood around my bed. I counted; seven of them this morning. Once again they pulled the sheets away from me and the curtain wasn't totally closed. I asked one of them to please close the curtain. They looked like, "Oh, well, OK." I decided that I was going to try to take some control over some of the things that I could: tell people to shut the curtains, and to not disrobe me quite so much. I felt exploited, so much like a specimen or a fish in a glass bowl.

Pretty soon a very tall gentleman in a dark suit came in. He started making gruff comments to the different residents, and asking them questions. It was obvious that he thought he was very important, but I wasn't sure I was too impressed at that moment. He left as gruffly as he came. The residents continued their probing and prodding and messing with the drains. One of them walked over to the window and opened up the blinds so they could see me, the specimen, a little bit clearer; the sunlight was coming in the window and it was at that point I realized that the construction elevator was right outside my window and was going upward. It was full of construction workers, men who had hard hats on with cigarettes dangling from their mouths. They looked shocked as they peered into my window. At that moment I felt horrible; I had again just lost control of who I was. I felt like my mind suddenly went up to the ceiling, leaving me depressed. I was on parade and wondered what those men thought as they looked in the window. Some of them just stared with their mouths hanging open. I watched them slowly rise up past the window. I truly felt like I couldn't handle anymore, turned my head away, and the tears slowly ran down into the pillowcase. The residents were totally oblivious to any feelings that I might be having. They attempted to cover me up and left. Again, they yelled, "If you need anything, let us know." I tried to straighten up the covers again, as best I could, and just laid there in a strange kind of shock.

They brought my breakfast in, but I wasn't hungry. I reminded the aide I couldn't open these things, my hands were too swollen. I realized my voice was almost angry, and I knew that I was still angry from what the residents had done with those men who continued to go up and down in the elevator. I felt like I was in a display cabinet.

After a while my nurse came in and said she was going to get me up for a bath today. I had not seen her before, she was a new one, tall with dark hair. In an authoritative voice she told me I was going to get out of that bed to get walking. I needed to go to a step-down unit and had to show that I was ready to go.

Her voice droned on and on and on, and I wondered how she thought I had been going to the bathroom. But I didn't say anything as I didn't have the strength to argue. She brought me a shallow basin of water, and I questioned why she was going to give me a bath with a cup full of water. Again I didn't say anything, I kept my mouth shut. She abruptly turned, pulled the curtains, and she said, "Let me know when you're done." Out the door she went.

I was mortified that she didn't even offer to help. What did she think I was going to do? I have this arterial line still in my left arm, and an IV in my right hand. I noticed that my IV was getting red, and was very sore and tender at the site. I looked at those swollen fingers and thought at least I could wash my face, hands, and do my armpits myself.

I realized she had undone my gown, and it fell all at once onto my lap. For the first time I saw my new breast I couldn't believe what I saw. It was just like a lump of flesh stuck on my chest. It was much larger than my other breast, and very bruised. It also had these tubes that came up from underneath my arms. I looked at it, a triangle-like patch of skin. It looked like it had been patched on with an extra piece of tissue sewn in. The incision line looked nice and clean but the new breast looked kind of flat, and had an odd shape as if it was just stuck on my chest. I didn't really know how I felt about it, but now it made me feel kind of sick. I suddenly realized that there were tears on my face, of which I didn't want any more.

I tried to wring the washrag out, but I couldn't do it. It was dripping water. The water was cool. I tried to get under my arm, but couldn't raise my left arm enough to get under there, and I couldn't use my left arm enough to get under the right one.. I didn't know if I was supposed to wash my chest or whatever, and my lap just seemed to get wetter the more I tried. I became more and more frustrated as I tried to wring the rag out.

I realized that there was some water sitting on my table, with my toothbrush and toothpaste sitting there, too. I thought I would clean my mouth and feel better.

I still smelled terrible, like a patient, and had this Intensive Care smell to my body that overwhelmed me. I looked at that lump of flesh on my chest, and that big incision on my belly, and the tubes, and the smell, and I just couldn't hold back any longer. I tried desperately not to, but the tears came.

The nurse came around from behind the curtain, looked at me and very coldly and asked just what I was crying about. I felt almost indignant as I responded. I thought I had a lot to cry about, and right now I want to cry and get this out of my system. I felt very frustrated, and I hated this feeling of helplessness.

She asked if I was done with my bath and her voice was so cold. I couldn't imagine where they found her. What made her so angry this morning? I certainly hadn't asked her to do anything for me but knew it would feel good to have my back washed off. That was a legitimate request.

I let her know I was done but could certainly use my back to be washed, and some lotion put on it too. My back hurt and I wasn't used to lying in bed. I felt achy all over. So she washed my back, and didn't say a word. I wondered what happened to warmed lotion as I always put the lotion in the warm water for my patients. I figured nobody ever taught her that.

I didn't really want to get into a confrontation with her, but did say I thought she had a problem with the IV. The areas was reddened and probably needed to be restarted. She responded, "Humph, why don't we start it in a little bit. Is it real painful?" I told her it wasn't yet, but I didn't want to get a phlebitis going. She said she didn't do them, the IV team would. I raised my voice and said I didn't care who did it, just so it was done.

She changed my bed and decided to get me up and walk me around in the room. We grabbed the IV pole and I held all my drains. We unhooked the arterial lines, and around the room I went. I felt pretty proud of myself after I had walked around, even though I still couldn't straighten up. I was pleased and thought I was making progress. She put me back to bed, and I put the TV on.

Another nurse came in and said in an irritated voice she was going to take out the art line and she had to hold it for five minutes. I suggested that while she was here, why didn't we get acquainted and talk a little bit. I asked her if they had a clinical nurse specialist in their unit. She told me her unit did have one but she had never seen her, she was always running around to meetings and never came to the unit.

I had watched her calibrate my art line and thought maybe I had hallucinated with the technique that they were using, but asked her about it. I asked what kind of policies and standardization did they have in the hospital? She told me each unit had their own standards and all did things differently. That's what made it so difficult. She hadn't wanted to come over today, her regular unit was somewhere else.

That explained a bit as to why she was not a happy camper that morning. She had been pulled to the burn unit. She went on and on at that point about how short staffed they were, how hard the work was, and how much time it took to do burn dressings, and nobody in administration ever looked at that, or thought about it.

She told me that they were going to stop my Demerol PCA pump, and that I could be started on oral pain medication. Inside I quietly thought how scary that was. I had done so well with Demerol, maybe I had used too much but didn't know. I wondered how I would get up and walk around without something for pain and I felt very uncomfortable. I really didn't want them to take the Demerol away. I felt tethered, it was my comfort, my "blankie," if you will. But she continued to hold pressure on the art line site. It felt good to get rid of another tube. It was another milestone in this journey from ICU to step-down.

Suddenly a very well dressed black woman came in the door. She had a frown on her face and started yelling at the nurse who was holding pressure on my art line. "Why has she still got that PCA pump? She's supposed to get that off. We've got to get her out of here. It's almost noon and she has to be out of here by 3:00 in the afternoon." The nurse just stood there and said she was holding pressure from removing the art line, and explained what she had done. The woman continued to yell, "I want her out of here by 3:00 p.m." I didn't know who that woman was, but I had a sneaky suspicion she was the head nurse. She never once looked at me, only yelled and talked very coldly to this nurse.

I asked quietly who she was and wasn't surprised to hear she was the nurse manager for the unit.

I knew that explained why there were so many nurses who came in and out of this unit, and none of them were really regular staff. I couldn't believe she talked like that in front of a patient. Maybe she had thought because I was a nurse I would understand, but I didn't. I never approved of anyone talking like that in front of a patient, regardless of what their staffing levels were, or what kind of pressure they were under. I really disliked her and heard her yelling at another nurse in the hall that she was taking too long to do a burn dressing. I knew I would never want to work there. I wouldn't care if they paid me triple time. I knew other patients heard her yelling at the nurses, too.

All morning I could hear that voice booming up and down the hall. She continued to tick me off I decided if she came back in my room, I would give her a piece of my mind and tell her that I thought she was a terrible nurse manager. I didn't care what was going on in the unit, nobody deserved to be treated or talked to like that.

My arm began to throb with its electric type pain, and I decided to take a little bit more of my Demerol as I knew I wasn't going to get anymore. I was going to have to get up and walk around and would be glad to be transferred out.

They woke me for lunch and I tried to eat again. It wasn't very good and the unidentified meat tasted dry.

Later the pain team and nurse came in, and out with the PCA pump they went. I had heard her yelling even more down the hall. Even though she had been cold to me, I realized that there were other reasons as to why she was acting the way she was. She came in and told me that my husband would be there, but she wanted to get the IV nurse in to change my IV before I was sent to step-down.

It was just a few moments and the IV nurse came in. She was going to pull the line from the back of my hand, and I talked her into switching it over to an intermittent IV device first, just in case she couldn't get it in. I knew they'd had lots of difficulties and had even stuck my feet sometime between the first surgery and the time I got to the burn unit, because I had seen the bruises where they had tried to get IVs in. So she did that, because we knew I'd have to have an IV for a while yet. She managed after a couple of sticks to get one in my upper arm.

Glenn came in and said they would be moving me in just a few minutes. So he helped gather up my stuff, put everything on the bed, and moved me in my bed. I looked around as we went down the hall, and thought they must really be full for the nurse manager to have been yelling like that. But there was a whole wing that was totally empty. Every bed was empty. There were only a few beds that actually had patients in them. I couldn't understand why that woman was so angry. I could see her sitting at the desk but she didn't even look up as I passed by. I felt like I wanted to stick my tongue out at her, but I thought that wouldn't be a very professional thing to do. But the thought did cross my mind.

CHAPTER TWELVE

Step-Down

The bumps were horrible as we went from one part of the building to the other. The nurse met me as I got off the elevator and said, "Welcome to our unit. We're so glad you're here." They checked me in, checked my blood pressure, my IVs and my flap. She seemed so professional, I was impressed and thought this woman had been more professional and thorough than most of the critical care nurses that I had had downstairs. I asked if at the change of shifts, she would be there.

She said she had been assigned just for the day, she was from another unit, and had come because they were short. I wondered if they had any real staff anywhere?

Soon another nurse came in who was very young and attractive. She had the shortest hair I had ever seen in real life, on a live person. She was cute, and had on a stripped top and white skirt. She looked more like she was ready to go play tennis than to do nursing care. She giggled at every other word, and laughed as she checked me in again.

She took my blood pressure, my temperature, and everything a second time. She was chattering away, but I couldn't understand what she was saying as she was talking so fast and so loud. She acted like I couldn't hear and it really bothered me.

She raised up my gown and looked at my new breast. Finally she said they told her she was supposed to look at the flap, but had never taken care of a patient like this. She hadn't the foggiest idea of what she was supposed to be looking for.

I thought wonderful, now here's someone who doesn't even know what she's supposed to be doing but I knew I had to give her another chance. I didn't need to be forming such fast first impressions.

We talked for a little bit, and I asked her about where she'd gone to school. She knew I was a nurse, and she'd made a couple of comments about taking care of a nurse, and was nervous about it. I tried to reassure her. I was truly not trying to make any judgments. Deep down inside, though, I couldn't help but make a few. She was truly trying very hard, and I could tell she was nervous. I caught her by the hand and told her not to worry about me. I agreed to put my light on if I needed her. If my light isn't on, I'll be fine. But if I put my light on, you'll know that I really need you."

We made a pact, because she was getting an admission that was unreal, they kept coming on the intercom. You're going to have an admission in number such and such a room, and she was going to take another admission an hour after that. This **was** a very busy unit.

The curtain was pulled between me and the bed next to the window. I knew there was a lady over there who must be very ill. I couldn't see her, but could hear her moaning in pain. I heard her ask for a shot. The nurse ran right out and came back with Demerol She said, "I have Demerol 75 mg for you. Roll over and I'll give it to you." In a little while there was no more moaning, and she was asleep.

I tried to watch TV and Glenn came back from eating. They brought me a tray and I ate. Glenn and I visited with each other and the evening passed all too quickly. I was tired but managed to learn my way back and forth to the bathroom with the help of my nurse. She was good to come and help me, and was warm and friendly. The only thing that bothered me was that she talked so loudly. But we got used to each other and I complained I wanted to wash my hair, it felt so dirty.

She said she would be on all this week and we would get the hair washed tomorrow night. She would help, did it all the time. She knew how she would feel if she had been in the hospital this long after surgery. She would want her hair washed too.

In a little while my roommate started moaning again, and the nurse came in and asked her the right kind of questions. The woman said her abdomen hurt so bad, she couldn't stand the pain any longer. The nurse went out and called the resident. He came in and started talking to her and away she went for some tests, some type of special abdominal x-ray. I dozed off and on, trying to watch some TV and I had a book to read and some magazines. The doctor had changed my pain medication to Tylox, an oral medication. I was nervous it might not work as well as the Demerol, even though I could have two at a time. The Tylox actually worked much better than the Demerol and I was quite impressed. I felt like I could move around a little bit more, and didn't feel quite so groggy. I could think more clearly.

My roommate however, continued to have a lot of pain. One of the residents came in about 10:30 p.m.. He started doing a complete history and physical right at the bedside. I could hear everything they said about the poor woman. I knew everything from her very first sexual experience to the one that she had right before she came into the hospital. I couldn't believe it, but it turned out that they diagnosed her with pelvic inflammatory disease. I wondered where was the confidentiality for this poor woman? And where's infection control?

Around midnight I was awakened by a very nice male nurse who was very caring. He asked me how I felt about having a male nurse take care of me and I told him I had no problem at all. I just wanted someone to take care of me, get well, and be able to get home as soon as possible. He not only introduced himself, he told me how long he'd been in nursing. He told me that it was his first time taking care of a patient with a flap. He explained that he would like to learn, and if I knew anything of what he was supposed to be looking for. I said I did, and explained to him how the skin would blanch. I became very technical and very much the teacher that I sometimes am.

He told me his wife was also a nurse. He was just so caring and easy when he pulled me up in bed. He was really concerned that I be comfortable. He had positioned the pillows and fluffed them, and even brought in two extra pillows for between my knees. Nobody had ever done that even in the ICU burn unit. He told me I needed a good nights sleep and if I needed anything, to let him know.

I slept very soundly for several hours, but all that fluid caught up with me, and I awoke suddenly realizing I had to get to the bathroom. I very quietly put the light on and waited. He appeared at the end of my bed and asked quietly what he could do for me. When I told him of my urgent need to go to the bathroom he quickly came around to the side of the bed. He practically lifted me out of the bed and stood me on my feet, and I shuffled to the bathroom. He waited on the outside.

I told him I was really impressed. He told me how he hadn't wanted to be anything else his whole life but a nurse. I shared with him that was how I felt. He fluffed all my pillows and tucked me back into bed, and emptied my tubes and my drains a little early, so he wouldn't bother me, and I could go back to sleep. I never saw him again..

I woke up early to hear my roommate moaning. She was really hurting, and was writhing in the bed. I felt very bad for her, her light was on and no one was coming. We sort of started talking together a little bit and I asked if there was anything I could do.

She said she had to have something for the pain, she couldn't stand it.

In a little while one of the nurses came in, answered her light, and she told her she'd go get something for pain. I told her since she was out there getting something for pain, if she wouldn't mind bringing me back just one Tylox. I said two makes me just a little bit too groggy, and I'd like to take a bath in a little bit. Could I just have one, and see if one would work?

She said sure.

She introduced herself when she came back in. She gave us our pain medication and I asked her if she'd set me up at the bedside and I would give myself a bath. The swelling had gone down in my hands, and I could actually wring the washrag. I could also wash my left armpit.

I began having an odd sensation in my new breast. I felt as if my old breast was back and it actually felt like the nipple was there. It was an odd feeling. I knew I had heard of phantom limb pain, but phantom boob pain?

One of the surgical residents came in and said he was going to pull two of the drains. One in the chest and one in the abdomen. The one thing that I had dreaded was having those drains pulled out. I wondered how painful it would be, and I really, truly regretted my decision to only take one Tylox. But I rolled over and gritted my teeth as he pulled the one under my arm first. I was kind of amazed, it didn't really hurt. It just sort of stung a little bit and seemed as if it took a long time to pull it out, but it didn't really hurt at all. So I didn't brace myself quite so much for the abdominal drain that he had started to pull. I couldn't believe how bad the pain was. It was amazing. I thought it had been clear down inside of me, and I just shuddered. He told the nurse to go ahead and give me another Tylox, and I drifted off to sleep.

Lunch came and I knew that the inevitable had arrived. I was going to need to get up and walk the hall. My nurse came by and she asked if I were ready. When I said yes, she sent in an aide and together we managed to get the drains pinned to my gown as I started walking. It wasn't very long until Glenn came and some friends from church. They couldn't believe that I was up walking around. I felt pale and wan and drained, but I knew I had achieved another real accomplishment. I don't know how I managed to get halfway down that hall and back without falling down, throwing up, or passing out. But I did.

Dr. Kurtzman came in that evening, and I sensed he was pleased with how well I was doing. I looked better, and I knew I felt better.

I remembered a friend of mine had told me how she had gotten up the day after her surgery, fixed her hair, and put on her make-up . I thought I would be lucky to even comb my hair, let alone put on make-up. But I thought maybe tomorrow I would feel like putting on some make-up. I took my Tylox that evening and went to sleep, hoping I would sleep all night.

I remembered the night nurse coming on and checking my drains. I remained in a dreamy state, and just barely remembered her. The next thing I knew they were bringing my breakfast tray in. It felt so good to have slept all night long, and not to have had all the interruptions or to have to get up and go to the bathroom. I could get myself to the bathroom now, without calling for help. All I had to do was carry my two drains, so I knew that I was getting better.

I still couldn't stand up straight, but I did go in the bathroom and give myself a bath that morning. There was a big sink in there, and I took the basin in, and made up some hot, sudsy water. I just sat on the toilet and washed and cleaned up. I put the basin down on the floor, stuck my feet in that warm water and it was great. I brushed my teeth and splashed water on my face. I even ventured out into the hall by myself. Maybe I really would live through this after all.

Dr. Kurtzman came in and asked me if I wanted to get rid of these tubes before I went home and of course I agreed. After all, I lived 45 minutes away. How would I get them out?

He said, "Well, we'll keep you a couple more days. Maybe on Friday we'll let you go home."

That felt good. Now I had a day I could think about as being able to go home.

Thursday morning I woke up on my own and listened as the breakfast trays came down the hall. I felt famished and ate every bit of my breakfast; I even ate the wallpaper paste cereal.

I got up and I put on a gown that buttoned down the front, and I went in the bathroom and took a complete bath. I realized there was a big angular spigot in there. As I was bent over all the time, anyway, I decided I could stick my head under there and washed my hair. I went back to bed and was drying my hair when the nurse came in. I admitted what I had done and even though I was tired, I felt better.

I took a Tylox. It didn't really help and a couple of hours later I was still hurting. My arm had that electric feeling, and I had forgotten to ask Dr. Kutzman about that. I knew it had been a couple of days since I had seen Dr. Hymes and would have to ask him. It was almost like my wish had come true as Dr. Hymes arrived. I told him about my arm, that electric pain, and how awful it was.

He assured me it was nerve pain and eventually would go away. But he also explained they had to remove the nodes and they were very close to the nerves. He had good news though. "Your nodes were negative," I heard him say it loud and clear!

That was one thing that I had just put out of my mind. I'd never asked what they were, I was just going to wait and let them tell me. They were negative. I felt now that my cancer was gone, I felt that I had the whole rest of my life ahead of me. I felt positive for the first time.

The plastic resident came in alone. He was tall and looked like Ichabod Crain. He checked me out and said it's time to get these drains out. Here we go again. The one in my abdomen was the most painful and it seemed even longer than the one the day before. As he pulled it out, the drainage came from around the puncture wound where it was. I continued to drain a lot that would last most of the day, even though they put dressings on it.

I continued to walk the halls as they told me. No one came to visit that afternoon but I had lots of phone calls, and talked on the phone for long periods.

My roommate was supposed to be going home. They had stopped her Demerol and told her she could be seen in the office.

I was hurting and had done a lot that morning. I would take another Tylox, if the nurse would bring it to me. I put my light on, and she said she couldn't give it to me, it wasn't time. It had not been four hours. I told her I was supposed to get **two** every four hours but had taken only one three hours ago. She refused again. I was upset and informed her I should be able to have another one since I hadn't taken two, but she refused again, only to take two Tylox over to my roommate.

About five minutes later, she came back and told my roommate and told her it was time to go home as she had been dismissed. How was she going to get home? My roommate told her she had her car in the parking lot and was going to drive home.

The nurse said, "OK, I'll get your papers and discharge ready."

I thought it wasn't quite right to give this lady two Tylox. She couldn't send her home. How could I tactfully tell this nurse that she can't send this woman home after giving her two Tylox, and expect her to drive home by her self?

The nurse came back in a few minutes, and I told her you can't send her home after giving her two Tylox. She couldn't let her drive that car. The nurse looked at me indignantly and said gruffly, "Why not?" And I answered, "You would be liable. You have given her controlled substance for pain, and you can't put her behind the wheel. If she has a wreck or kills herself or someone else..."

She responded she had never heard that and my mind just started going like a mile a minute and I said, "That's the law." I asked her how long had she been a nurse and she answered for seven years. She walked out of the room muttering as she left and I could tell I had really made her angry.

It wasn't five minutes later that the resident came fuming in but by that time my roommate was sound asleep. He asked who had given her the Tylox and the nurse answered he had ordered them. When she wanted something for pain that was what was given. Everybody was mad, and they both glared at me as they walked out of the room. My roommate ended up staying in the hospital another day. Finally I convinced a nurse to give me another Tylox, and I slept most of the afternoon.

My Mom called and said she wouldn't come down today. I was waiting for Glenn to come and Dr. Kurtzman was due in anytime. In a few minutes I saw Glenn's smiling face come in and I was proud because I had clean hair, and a little bit of make-up.

Glenn had been there only a few minutes, when my roommate's family arrived. Her sister and brother-in-law came, brought her two children, plus their own two children, and her boyfriend also arrived. The children kept running back and forth and the room was too small for all of these people. It all just made me more and more tired. They took the chair that Glenn was sitting in, and he had to sit at the end of my bed.

When Dr. Kurtzman came in, Glenn was sitting at the end of the bed and the children were running and talking loudly. Dr. Kurtzman asked me if I'd walked in the hall. I told him all I had accomplished. He looked at me and agreed to send me home the next day but about that time, one of those little children went darting past. He looked behind the curtain, saw all those people there, looked at Glenn and I, asked if I wanted to make it tonight? Glenn and I looked at each other and I said 'Yes.' I would go home in a split second.

I couldn't believe I was going home. I was thrilled and Glenn was happy. He helped pack me up. The little nurse that I'd had the first night was on, the one who had promised to wash my hair. She came in and said she was getting ready to check me in for the 3-11 shift and she said she was going to wash my hair. She had been too busy the night before. I her not to feel badly and showed her the job I had done on my hair myself that morning. We all laughed at my accomplishment.

She offered to help with the discharge process and get the paperwork started right away, get the prescriptions in order, and make sure everything was OK. When she came back, she had a ton of paperwork. I never saw as much paperwork as I had to do to get out of that place.

She sat down to give me the discharge instructions and I used the opportunity to tell her that I would like to have an exit interview. She wrote down some of the things that I felt were just not right during my stay.

I talked about the nurse coming in and leaving me lay in the fluid and about her pulling on my Foley, almost pulling it out. I talked about the nurse who didn't offer to help me with my bath and how I couldn't do things for myself. I told them about an incident that I'd had with someone out at the front desk on that unit when I asked them to empty my roommate's urine, they told me to empty it, I was a nurse, I knew how to do intake and output. I said I wasn't a nurse, I was not being paid to empty my roommate's urine. I had to go, and I wasn't about to do it. Yet, because I had to go so badly, I ended up at least sitting it on the floor. I felt that it was inappropriate that they would put a new surgical patient in with someone who had pelvic inflammatory disease, and allow us to use the same bathroom, if there were other empty beds available, which I knew there were. She was nice, and wrote everything down that I said, but I was ecstatic just to be going home.

I was very happy, until I realized that my husband had come to get me in his Camaro. Camaro's are known for their fast ride, not necessarily their smooth ride. The streets of Cincinnati were full of potholes, I knew it would be a bumpy ride home, but didn't care. The trip home was very slow. I just was miserable every time he would hit any kind of a bump as it would shoot pains all through my body.

When I saw the house, there was nothing in the world so sweet as my home. I was so very glad to be there. I headed straight for my blue sofa, and parked my fanny there, putting my legs up. I didn't move for two hours, just sat there, so glad to be home. Melissa was there and it was quiet. It was wonderful!

I was a little nervous about going up the stairs the first time as I hadn't practiced them. When it came time for bed, I knew that I had to go up these stairs and it was difficult and very painful, even after taking a Tylox. I got upstairs and thought why I had only taken one. I was going to take two. When I got up there I also realized I didn't know how to lay down in the bed. I hadn't really laid completely flat and always had the head of the hospital bed up.

Glenn propped two or three pillows up, But I still couldn't get down. I didn't have anything to hold on to and needed a side rail. I became so frustrated, and he didn't know what to do to help me, as I still couldn't get down to the bed. It hurt too bad. We struggled, but I still couldn't lay down. I wasn't too good at laying on my left side anyway, and I was trying to get in on what was 'my side' of the bed. We finally figured out if we put a chair there I could use that and it worked pretty well.

Pretty soon Glenn came to bed and I realized that this must be very difficult for him. I couldn't even turn my head to give him a kiss goodnight, but he said he was glad to have me back home.

Sometime during the night I had a terrible nightmare and couldn't decide if it was real or a nightmare, as it seemed so real. I was home, could see the bedroom, but the closet door was open, and there was a big flame in the closet. I couldn't tell if it was real, and I couldn't talk. I couldn't make my voice loud, it was like a little whisper that came out. Suddenly, it was as if the devil was standing next to me, and he was trying to get me to go into the closet. Well, I could see that the closet really wasn't the closet, it was a furnace and the devil was trying to push me into it, but I kept saying, no.

Glenn woke me up and said I was having a nightmare. I thought it seemed so real. I really was very upset and frightened. The closet door was standing wide open. I always liked to shut the closet door, because I was always afraid I'd run into it in the middle of the night.

I got up and used the bathroom, and came back to bed. It took me about ten minutes to get back down again. Glenn was wide awake, and I felt bad for him. He had taken the next day off, because he had thought I'd be coming home, so I knew he didn't have to get up real early. We lay there for a little while and though he tried to hold me, I really couldn't stand for him to touch me. I hurt all over and wasn't used to having anybody in bed. Every time he would roll over I would hurt. I lay there for quite a while, trying to go back to sleep.

Finally, I went back to sleep, but I had another dream. I dreamt I was in bed and there were snakes on the floor, and I was trying to go to the bathroom. I was trying to climb on my chair, but I couldn't get the snakes away from the floor or from the chair. I was crying and yelling again, and Glenn once again was waking me up. I told him there were snakes on the floor but he assured me I was having another bad dream. I thought the night would never end and felt more exhausted when the morning came than before I went to bed.

Glenn fixed a wonderful breakfast and I ate his delicious french toast, the best in the whole world. I had decided I would go down the stairs once in the morning, and go up once at night and sometime during the morning, my Mom came. Liz brought lunch, a wonderful chicken dish and it tasted fantastic. Liz left, my Mom stayed and fixed dinner. I could tell that the healing had begun.

Around bedtime I became frightened of going to bed. The Tylox worked wonderfully during the day, but I wondered of it could have given me the nightmares the night before. I only took one, but again I couldn't sleep for the nightmares: fires and houses burning down. I was running from monsters that were huge, bigger than houses. They were chasing me, and grabbing me. I was frightened, couldn't sleep, couldn't turn in the bed. I was uncomfortable, miserable and hated the night. I would try to force myself to stay awake, but the darkness just seemed to swallow me up into a fit of nightmares.

The next day was Saturday and Melissa was home. Once again I wanted Glenn's french toast. I watched TV and went to sleep, I was so tired. Glenn woke me up for a bit of lunch, and I went back to sleep and I slept again. I woke for supper and the church had brought a wonderful meal. I ate and ate, the beef, corn, and the cake were so tasty. The doorbell kept ringing with people bringing food, and it was generous of everyone, but I was tired, I didn't feel like visitors.

Once again nighttime came, and I became more and more frightened. I didn't want to take the Tylox at all, but I knew I couldn't stand the pain. I couldn't sleep without something. I thought about calling Dr. Kurtzman, but didn't want to bother him because of this. I slept all night and didn't have one nightmare.

I woke up on Sunday morning feeling better but moving very slowly. That afternoon I had lots of phone calls from people from church, my friend Nancy called, my Mom came over, and my sister came over. Ashley and Ryan brought me gifts, and my pastor came and had prayer with me. We were so grateful and so thankful for how far I had come.

That evening I was sitting on the sofa, watching a little TV with the family, when the phone rang around 10:00 p.m.. It was Dr. Kurtzman. He called to see if I was 'minding' him, and to see if I was doing what he told me to do. He really was just checking up on me, making sure that I didn't have any problems. I'd never had a doctor call me at home and ask how I was doing. I knew that he really cared about me and what I was going through. How much I appreciated him!

Monday came, and it was another busy day. My Mom came over and stayed with me as Glenn tried to do some work. I called my grandparents and tried to return some of the calls from people who had called me. The flowers started coming and I got them from Kim and Rob, my Sunday School class, from where Glenn worked. My house began to look like a florist shop there were so many. Every day more flowers came from people at work, friends and neighbors. A big fruit basket came that was absolutely beautiful from my dear friend Bobbie and her family. My neighbors next door brought over a meal and the best brownies I think I've ever eaten in my life. The church even sent food over. Food seemed to be coming out our ears and we certainly weren't going hungry.

Time was beginning to pass very quickly as I began to do things more and more for myself. I was growing stronger every day. I learned to lay in the bed and get up and down without having help, or using the chair. I was learning to take care and take control of my life again. I had to go see Dr. Kurtzman and Dr. Hymes on Tuesday. They set the appointments up so I could see one right behind the other. They were real pleased at how well I was doing. I was moving slow, but getting better.

Tuesday afternoon Glenn had to go see Dr. Ongkiko for his yearly appointment and I was determined to go with him. Dr. Ongkiko hadn't known I had surgery for cancer. He expressed his sympathy, and truly seemed to care about what our family was going through, so soon after Glenn's illness.

All that week flowers continued to come, until the family room was totally full. I couldn't believe how many people supported and cared about me. My cousin Linda called almost every night, and we would talk and it was like old times as we were more like sisters than cousins. Life was beginning to take on a meaning that would provide me with a new hope for the future.

CHAPTER THIRTEEN

Hair Today, Gone Tomorrow

I knew I had to decide about where to do my chemotherapy, whether to do it here in Middletown with Dr. Malcolm or go to Cincinnati. I talked to Dr. Hymes and he had made an appointment with me to go down and see another oncologist on Thursday. He was very nice, but offered me some treatments that seemed a little different than what Dr. Malcolm had offered. I called Dr. Malcolm back and he said he would do some research, and get back with me as to what would be the most standard treatment for a woman with my kind of cancer.

In the meantime the other oncologist had told me that he had a new chemotherapy nurse, and he wanted me to meet her. She was from Dayton, and thought maybe I would know her. When he gave me her name I was stunned, she was the one nurse I had feared my whole life. I had done some oncology nursing about ten years before, and I knew I would never want her to take care of me in any way, shape or form But here she was, taking care of patients right where I would be a patient. I told him straight out I couldn't do that, I could not let that woman touch my body, let alone give me chemotherapy. I didn't want to give him too terrible of an impression, but I told him I felt that the Lord had led me to stay in Middletown, and that's why I would go to Dr. Malcolm.

I called Dr. Malcolm's office and talked with Susan, his nurse, to see when I was to see them. I went in and he provided me with all kinds of evidence that the best treatment for my kind of cancer was indeed what they called polychemotherapy. I would be placed on Cytoxin, Methyltrexate, and 5FU. That was the standard treatment across the country and I would receive it every three weeks with blood counts in between. I said that if we could do it on Fridays, that would be the best for my work schedule as I wanted to go back to work. Both doctors had told me that chemotherapy didn't make people as sick anymore and that most people worked right through. I agreed that on September 3rd, a Friday, I would start. That was just a little over three weeks after my surgery.

I was walking upright now, and feeling pretty good. I still couldn't wear a bra, and my side was still very numb, my arm was numb, and I was plagued with those electric-like pains that had not really left. They said that sometimes women had to put up with these for several months and that they would eventually dissipate, but I showed no signs of relief. I only spent two weeks on the Tylox, then had switched to Nuprin, and could tolerate the pain. I remember one instance of going with my family to the Dairy Queen. I carried my arm close to my body, as if to protect this mound of flesh, and my sister said I looked like a stroke patient. I immediately put my arm down to my side and tried to carry my body in a more normal alignment. It caused the pain to be a little worse, but I certainly didn't want to look like a stroke patient. I did appreciate Shawn telling me this.

September third came all too quickly. I hoped to start back to work as soon as I got one or two treatments completed. I was anxious to go back and get into a normal routine. I thought it would help me get away from some of the feelings of sadness that still haunted me in quiet moments.

I remember meeting Susan that day in the office, and she took me back to the chemo room. It was done in a Colonial Style, with a dark green leather chair, plaid wallpaper, and very attractive drapes, supposedly homey. Green was never one of my favorite colors, and as I walked in and I saw that big leather chair, I felt like I wanted to throw up, and I hadn't even had the chemotherapy yet. Susan sat me down, and explained what she would do. Dr. Malcolm came in and he sat and talked with us throughout the treatment.

Susan told me each drug she gave me. As she gave me one drug she told me that it would make me feel as if I had just been slammed in the nose. I thought, yeah, I wonder what that's going to feel like, slammed in the nose. I couldn't believe it, but it was just like she said. I felt like somebody had indeed punched me in the nose, but it didn't last very long. I felt a little bit nauseated, but they had a new drug that they gave me prior to the chemo, called Zofran. It had just come out in December of 1990, to alleviate any nausea. Sure enough I didn't get nauseated or vomit. I felt a little gaggy a couple of times, but nothing too bad.

I got through the treatment, and when I got back to our house, Liz and Bruce were in the driveway wanting to go out and get something to eat. I thought I felt well enough to do that and saw no reason not to.

Saturday morning they had advised me to take part of the Zofran by mouth. They had put it into a couple of doses, and I was to take one in the morning. I took it, and I didn't feel too bad. Along towards afternoon, I started feeling real tired, and much more nauseated than I had before. I went to bed early, only to wake up again with dreams of being on fire, only this time it was true. I really felt that there was a fire in my chest. My throat truly felt inexplicably as if it was on fire. I couldn't lay down; I couldn't sit up, I was miserable. I had some Mylanta left over from years ago in the cabinet and drank almost the whole thing. It gave me a few minutes of relief, but didn't last very long.

I got up the next morning and called Dr. Malcolm right away. He ordered me some Tagamet. It helped tremendously. I knew I would just have to stay on Tagamet throughout all of the treatments, as sometimes that happens.

They told me I wouldn't lose all my hair, but that I might lose some of it, to be prepared between days 10 and 14. Day 10 came and went, and I still had plenty of hair. I didn't notice any of it falling out, and was thrilled. Glenn and I discussed that maybe I should go ahead a get a wig, just in case. Something had told me maybe I should be prepared so I had called a place in Dayton. A man named Bill answered the phone, and was very helpful. He said he would see about fitting me for a wig as there are a certain percentage of people who will lose their hair. I asked my friend Kim if she would drive up there with me, so she met me one day after work, and we went in. She helped me get styled and get the wig. When they first put it on my head, it was very, very long. I made the comment that I looked like the original Loretta Lynn, but he cut, and styled, and soon I looked like Sue with a wig on. I don't think anybody would ever really knew I had a wig, unless I told them. It looked real, but I felt like I had a hat on, so I put it away until, and if, the day would arrive that I might need it.

I remember the day well. It was the 21st of September. I was going to Zanesville to my cousin's wedding and went into the shower to wash my hair. I didn't think too much about it as I put my hands in my hair. When I took my hands out, they were full of hair. My wedding rings were just covered and it was as if some kind of animal had been killed, and the fur was all in my hands. I realized that the hair was also on my shoulders and on my arms, and the shower was full of hair. As I rinsed and tried to get it off, more hair seemed to fall out. I couldn't believe it, and thought I might feel panicky, but I didn't. I just couldn't get it off. I couldn't get it out of the shower, it was just gobs and gobs of hair. I wondered what I would look like when I came out. I grabbed a towel and dried my body off as best I could, and put on my underwear. I called for Glenn and I looked in the mirror. There was still hair on my head, but there was also hair all over my arms. He worked with me, and together we plucked it off of my body where it had stuck to my wet skin. When he opened the shower, it was unreal. Even he was shocked to see how much hair was all over the shower. It just seemed to be everywhere in the bathroom.

I quickly dried my hair to see how much I would have left. Maybe I would have to start wearing that wig but my hair didn't look too bad. We were kind of amazed, and Glenn said he thought I could go a couple more weeks, maybe one more treatment. I didn't cry. By this time the tears were pretty much gone and I had sort of accepted what I had to go through.

I was happy and excited about going to the wedding. I got on the scales that morning, and had lost about four pounds. I was quite slim, as slim as I'd been in a long time. I felt pretty good and my hair looked good.

I sat on pillows all the way to Zanesville and it was a beautiful wedding. It was so good to see some of my family, my grandparents, my aunts and uncles, and my cousin Linda. I hadn't seen my cousin Kelley in a long time and she was a beautiful bride. Her new husband, Rich seemed to fit in the family just wonderfully.

I was tired by the end of the wedding, and I'd made a brief appearance at the reception as Glenn and I drove home that evening, I was glad to begin to lead a normal life. Little did I know it would be another year before my life would be normal again.

CHAPTER FOURTEEN

Nurses Don't Get Constipated

My blood counts were too low by the time my second chemo treatment rolled around. Instead of being a three week cycle, it was now going to be a four week cycle. I was angry as I wanted to get it over. I had my calendar all made out, that I would be finished with chemotherapy by the end of January, and didn't want to have to push it back even one week. I was angry and frustrated. I called my friend Liz, and I almost cried on the phone with utter, complete despair. I wanted the chemo treatment to be over with. I wanted to get on with my life, but that wasn't the way it was going to be.

After my second treatment, I woke up with some severe cramping in my abdomen. I realized that I hadn't gone to the bathroom and my bowels hadn't moved in about six days. It seemed odd that I just never felt the urge. I felt terrible, sick, and more nauseated than ever. I didn't know what to do. I called Dr. Malcolm to ask him if there should be a certain kind of laxative that I should take and he put me on pericolace. I had been taking Colace a stool softener, off and on since surgery because of the extensive work in my abdomen. I just didn't have the urge. It was like nothing. My abdomen was silent except for some very severe cramping very high up. I went to the pharmacy, got a fleet enema, and started taking the Pericolace, but nothing happened. Two days later I called him back and still nothing happened. My bowels felt like they'd been turned off. He told me to take more Pericolace. Finally I went a little bit, and got some relief. I was taking five pericolace a night, and getting a little bit of results with that. I began to think of myself as sometimes we nurses think of our older patients, as "bowel fixated". How awful that sounded to me. I was uncomfortable all the time, and I didn't care if I was becoming "bowel fixated.".

I was able to work a few days, but the nausea and the pressure got to me. I took a day off in between my days that I would be working and took an enema. I thought I would get some relief, but not very much. I called Dr. Malcolm back, and he said to take two more Pericolace. It was almost time for my next treatment, and I knew that I had to get my system going, or it would be worse. I took another fleet enema, and finally got some relief. I worked for three days, it was time for another treatment.

I went in and he asked me how my bowels were doing and I admitted, not very well and I had to take three enemas. He told me I could continue to increase the Pericolace and wrote an order for something called Cronulac. He told me to take this medication for <u>severe</u> constipation I took my treatment, and was very sick.

While Dr. Malcolm was out of town, I got flu-like symptoms. I ached all over and got a very bad sore throat. His office nurse told me if I developed a fever of 100 or greater to call. When my temperature reached 101, I called the office. They referred me to one of his associates. The doctor saw me in the middle of the day, gave me some medicine and antibiotics, and told me if I wasn't better in 24 hours or if my temperature went over 101, to call her back. All night long I was miserable. My temperature didn't really go over 101. It stayed that way, and I just stayed home and kept fighting this terrible cold and flu-like symptoms.

Once again I found that my bowels weren't working, so I went up to ten Pericolace and nothing happened. Two days of ten Pericolace, still silence, nothing. Only I felt distended and sore, just utterly and completely miserable. I took some of the Cronulac that Dr. Malcolm had ordered for me. I had results and I felt better. I kept thinking this would pass and all would start going again. I felt a little better, and went in to work for a few days.

It was a busy time at work. My manager had asked me if I would do a research survey and duplicate a study of professional uniforms for nurses in our hospital. She gave me a journal article as reference and I would try to duplicate the study over the next few months. I realized that I had to put together a whole questionnaire and figure out a way to do sampling. I was tired and fatigued and I didn't even know if I could think straight. I considered it a challenge, and continued to work on it. They were operating with a short time frame and wanted it done quickly. I began work on it, but all the time I became more and more plagued with the fatigue and symptoms from the chemotherapy.

I still didn't go to the bathroom, was regularly taking ten Pericolace every day, but it didn't work. I would go maybe twice a week. I got into a regime of taking that every day, then every Wednesday and Sunday I would take Cronulac. I could manage that without feeling too distended or too uncomfortable.

It was November by then and Glenn and I focused on Melissa's 21st. birthday. She had returned to her studies at Miami University and was working part time at a local department store. Melissa was very supportive of me during my chemotherapy treatments, bringing home brightly wrapped packages containing whimsical ceramic animals. These gifts were representative of the growing bond developing between us. God was giving us these special moments.

I noticed that I was beginning to put on a few pounds and decided it was from one of the medications, Decadron. My face was getting rounder and my body seemed to be getting thicker. My clothes were fitting tight, but I could still get into them. I knew that I would probably gain some weight, so I just kind of put it out of my mind, and continued to focus on her birthday. We had planned a surprise birthday party, and we had invited some of her friends, and told her friends to invite other friends. On Melissa's birthday, we had someone take her to the mall, and then bring her back to our house We told her we'd have some cake and ice cream at our house with her Grandmother. We had people park down around the corner, and when she arrived I think we had truly surprised her, especially when everyone jumped out and yelled, "Surprise!" We had a 21-balloon salute and lots of cake and ice cream, a fun time.

My third chemotherapy treatment had been put on hold again, because my counts were too low, I was being held up another week and it seemed my cycles were not going to be three weeks apart, but four, which only made the chemotherapy longer. Glenn and I would look at each other and say, "When the tulips bloom you'll be finished with the chemotherapy," but it seemed such a long way off, and my energy level was decreasing day by day.

By the end of November I had pretty much put the uniform study together, and also finished up all the critical care policies and procedures for the year. I knew December would be an easier month, that not much would be going on because of the holidays. I had hopes that maybe I could just start the new year with a renewed exuberance, if I could just muster up the energy to get through Thanksgiving and Christmas.

It was the week before Thanksgiving and we discovered quite by accident that Vere and Diane had invited the entire family up for Thanksgiving. They invited Glenn's mom and dad, and with Glenn's mother in failing health, it was so good to know that she could make the trip to Middletown. Diane had invited some of her family, Suzanne, Larry and Van. Everybody but us and my feelings were hurt, I could hardly function. It seemed to take what little bit of energy I had. I'd lay awake at night, crying. I didn't want Glenn to see my tears. I thought maybe I had said or done something to make her angry, or to hurt her feelings. I would wrack my brain until the wee hours of the morning, trying to think what I could have done to make her so angry, she couldn't even invite us to dinner at her home. She'd been at our house so many times for dinner, but yet we had never been invited to theirs. Never had I eaten anything but dessert there once, a long time ago.

I became so despondent and depressed that Glenn finally called Vere and asked him what the problem was. Why weren't we invited? He responded that nothing was wrong. They came over one evening, and we got a half of an invitation to come over if we wanted to the next day. We'd already made our own plans, and it was really after the fact. My Mom was going to come over and help cook and actually did most of it.

Liz's mother had gone to be with her sister who recently had a baby, so Liz, her Dad and Bruce decided to come over and eat Thanksgiving dinner with us. Thanksgiving morning I got a phone call from Liz, that she was sick with the flu and couldn't come over, but Bruce and John did. My Mom was here, and Shawn, Will and the kids came over for a little while later in the day. We all enjoyed Thanksgiving.

Glenn's Mom, Dad, Suzanne, Larry and the boys came over and visited for a little while. I still felt sad and wondered what I had done to put such an alienation in the family. Glenn seemed to be taking it well, but I could tell that at night his jerking was worse. By this time I had gotten used to the jerking that he did at night. I would almost wake up

111

when he stopped, rather than when he started. It was funny how we had gotten used to things. Glenn had gotten used to me being able to lay only on one side. But slowly and surely I began to be able to turn from side to side, and roll around the bed like a normal person.

Our love life was not worth a whole lot during these months. I was so tired and fatigued it was nearly non-existent. I would wonder how he could keep going on with someone like me, who's so tired, and hurting and aching all the time. What kept him here and keeps him coming home? He's a handsome man and could have any woman he wanted, but yet he kept coming home to me. He kept telling me he loved me, and he'd hold me. I felt so unworthy of all the love and adoration that I knew he gave me. I felt bad about the rift with his family, and wondered it I had been the cause of it. I loved him so much, more than I could even imagine.

The Lord had been good to us, but the last few months had been hard. It was a struggle for me to go from day to day. Some days I was so tired I couldn't even think about getting to the bathroom. I would lay on the sofa and I pray for help to walk to the bathroom. I was so tired, I didn't know how much more I could take. The days were often long and lonely. I would put the TV on just to have some noise in the house. I wondered why my Mom wouldn't drive over and just visit with me, but knew she had to take care of my sister's children. Sometimes I just wanted her to come over and surprise me and say, "I just came to visit. I just came to see you." But she didn't.

I became very depressed. On the days that I was home, I became a person who just walked the rooms of my house. My house didn't seem like a home and it didn't seem a friendly place. It was a place where I was sick and held captive by my illness. I felt like a prisoner. I couldn't get out and I didn't feel like it anyway. I knew I had to change my attitude and change what was happening in me. I began to pray, "Dear Lord, give me a more positive outlook." The end of this **would** happen, chemotherapy **will** end. My life **would** come back together again. I prayed for Him to give me strength and courage.

It was almost like a miracle, that first week in December.

I started thinking about Christmas presents and Christmas day, and what I could do to maybe bring Glenn's family back together again. What could I do that would help us to feel the good times like we had in the past? The first week in December Melissa and I wrapped the Christmas presents. We brought all the Christmas decorations up, and slowly, over a period of several days, managed to get them all up. The house seemed more friendly and festive with the decorations up, and I felt more positive than I had in weeks. My strength wasn't there, and I really wasn't able to work more than a day or so a week, but I managed to crawl in and do something.

I focused mostly on what I could do to rebuild the relationship in Glenn's family. I had decided that I would try to have a Christmas get together. I called all the family and invited them over for the 27th of December. I told them that I wouldn't put a lot of work into it and I would order out. But we would all get together and open presents like we had done in the past. I knew I didn't have the strength to travel to Glenn's parents, and I also knew I couldn't take the risk of going out. My blood counts were very low and I didn't need anymore illnesses. There were lots of different kinds of flu going around and I didn't want to be exposed, so I wasn't working or doing much of anything the middle weeks in December. But I felt happy as I planned for the dinner.

Christmas day arrived and we opened our packages, but I did not feel real well. I was trying to save up what little bit of energy I had for the 27th. My Mom, Shawn, Will, Ryan and Ashley all came over, and we opened our presents. We had a very enjoyable day. However, I went to bed early and thanked the Lord for the goodness that He'd given us for that day.

I focused on the 27th. I got up early and fixed what little bit of hair I had left. It was pretty thin, but some of the bald spots had started to grown in. It looked like a 9:00 shadow growing in. I knew things were getting better when you start growing hair.

I was happy that morning as I prepared the meal. It wasn't long before Suzanne and Larry arrived with Glenn's parents. Van came, and we anxiously waited to see if Vere and Diane were going to come. We finally called them, and they said they were putting in a kitchen sink, and weren't coming over. I felt so sad and heart-broken I could hardly go on. But I was glad for the fact that Glenn's Mom and Dad were there.

We opened all of our presents, but Vere and Diane's presents remained unopened under the tree throughout the entire Christmas season. They didn't come over, and New Year's Day came and went without hearing from them. I finally put those presents underneath the cabinets in the kitchen, wondering if they would ever come over again, and if we would ever be able to mend the relationship. I knew that Glenn was very saddened by this. He wouldn't talk about it very much, but when he did he kept saying, maybe in the spring things will get better, when I was through with chemo. But I could see the sadness in his eyes.

CHAPTER FIFTEEN

Home Bound

The New Year came and went and we managed to get the Christmas decorations down, and I got through another chemo treatment. But I was sicker than I had ever been before. I felt bad because in December I had heard about one of our nurse managers at the hospital who had been diagnosed with breast cancer, also. She was younger than I, only 37, and she had two little ones at home. It just tore at my heart that another woman that I had felt close to was having to go through this same thing. At least my daughter was grown. Here she was, young and with babies, facing this. She'd had her mastectomy on Christmas Eve. My heart just ached for her. I sent her cards and let her know that I was thinking of her. I sent her some samples from my Mary Kay collection and I put her on our prayer list in my Sunday School class.

Throughout all this madness I had managed to teach two out of every three Sundays of my class. The class had such a camaraderie, and love for the Lord that we couldn't stop meeting. I couldn't give up the teaching. It is in cases like this that the teacher was learning more than the pupils. The lessons I was learning from the Bible were the lessons I needed to learn to get from day to day. I was learning to lean upon the Lord to get through this intense fatigue that seemed to hold my body.

I had now gained over 35 pounds. My ankles and my feet hurt all the time and my legs were so heavy that my thighs were rubbing together and I was getting sores. I had mouth sores almost all the time and was plagued with very severe conjunctivitis. I would wake up in the morning and my eyes would be red with drainage coming out of the corners. I couldn't see and it seemed that my vision got worse and worse. I tried to work a couple of days, but really couldn't remember the things I'd done. I was tired beyond anything I had ever been before and my body felt huge and unfamiliar with the severe weight gain. I was depressed.

I didn't want to go anywhere, I didn't want to see anybody but my family. I didn't want anyone else to see me. I just wanted to hibernate in the house on the sofa. I was so sick some days that I really didn't do anything but literally lay on my sofa and listen to Oprah and Maury Povich. It seemed these two shows would allow me to escape some of the pain I was going through.

My Mom called almost every day, but always asked me how I was feeling. If I really told her how sick I was, she would respond that she felt as if she was going through chemotherapy too. I realized that Mom was going through an emotional chemo, too, but her statements always made me feel sad. She seemed so alone during this time. She had been depressed since my father was killed in 1983, and I knew she had never gotten over it. I couldn't help her then and I couldn't help her now. For some strange reason we couldn't comfort each other very well even though we wanted to.

I felt more and more depressed, sometimes lashing out at Glenn and Melissa, only because I was so fatigued and angered by what was happening to me and to my body. I felt as though I had lost everything. I couldn't think and I couldn't see. I looked horrible, my hair had gone. But yet deep down inside there was something that kept saying I had to keep going, this too shall pass. In the spring the tulips **would** bloom again. I felt almost schizophrenic, part of me would try to be positive and think ahead, but part of me couldn't think beyond the next five minutes.

It was a dreary time after the holidays. Our friends went to Vail skiing. I felt even more cheated and angry inside. This awful disease had invaded my body without permission and I was angry at myself for being depressed. Something inside told me that I had to somehow become more positive with my life. So when I would go out on those brief occasions and people would look at me like I had never had anyone look at me before, I would think to make a joke and say something funny.

I couldn't wear any of my real clothes and had gone to mostly sweatsuits. I had gone to the real cheap stores and bought great big sweatsuit tops that came almost to my knees, trying to hide some of the largeness and the fat. I would make jokes to people, saying I had put on so much weight so fast that my feet and ankles don't know what to do. They look up at me and ask, what happened up there? I would laugh and people would laugh, and would wonder how I could keep my humor. Secretly inside I knew it was good for me. I'm not sure if it was that funny, but if it made other people feel more comfortable around me I would say it.

I really did have difficulties getting in and out of the car. I felt like I was walking like I did when I was nine months pregnant, only I was almost 26 pounds over what I ever was at nine months plus pregnancy. I was very uncomfortable. I was short of breath a lot of times, with energy expended. Dr. Malcolm and Susan, his nurse, would weigh me and say I could get it off when the chemotherapy was over.

I truly felt I couldn't do any more chemotherapy, and became more and more concentrated on the fact that my body wasn't going to take anymore. I would wake up at night feeling short of breath. I didn't know you could even feel like that. I had a new insight for some of our patients who are so short of breath. I had to sleep on more and more pillows, in a more and more propped position. Glenn's and my sex life was practically nil. How could I feel sexy when I was so huge? Why would he even want someone who looked like me? I had some hair, a turkey topknot that stood straight up. And it truly did, no matter what I would do, it would never lay down. The bald spots were everywhere: in the very back, along my neckline, there was a long row that had grown real long and that had never come out for some strange reason. The remainder of the early bald spots were covered with a gray 5:00 shadow.

I didn't feel sexy at all, but yet I knew that Glenn knew that I needed him and he needed me in some strange way. We managed to let each other know that. Snuggling and cuddling became a real big part of our life, because the energy just wasn't there to go through making love. I felt sorry for him, and my heart went out to him. I tried to be so kind to him in a lot of other ways.

My anger and frustration continued to haunt me. It seemed to stem sometimes from just little things. My Mom would call and she'd say that she and Shawn had gone out to eat lunch. They had never invited me, I would be angry and think just one time, why couldn't they invite me? I knew that I probably couldn't go, but they could invite me, but never did. It seemed that my feelings got hurt a lot, and I cried. We never heard from Glenn's family. His sister Suzanne didn't call, his Mom never called, although we would frequently call her and check on her condition to see how she was doing. So we knew pretty much what was going on with them. Glenn's brothers never called and my sister never called. It was a very dark and bleak time.

Once in a while the Pastor or Terry would stop by, but it always seemed to be late in the evening when I had taken my hair off, and I just didn't want anyone to see me without it. One time Liz invited Glenn and I over for a birthday dinner for a friend of ours and she had a very nice dinner.

I had managed to go to the mall and brought a big woman sized hot pink kind of a knit suit. The sleeves were much too long for my petite body, and I rolled them up several times. But the top was long and came to my knees, and I felt like it hid some of the fat. When I put it on I realized I had gained even more weight than when I had bought it. It fit tighter across my rump and rode up, but I wore it anyway. I put my wig on, the one thing that still managed to look nice. Kim would keep it washed and set for me, and that was about the only thing that made me feel human.

We went to dinner, and I had an OK time. But I felt so fat and ugly, it was hard and we went home early. I cried on the way home and I couldn't understand why I cried so much. It seemed that tears were probably the only thing that I had a lot of these days. The weather was gloomy and dreary, too. It didn't snow, it just rained. And the rain just made me more and more gloomy.

I called and told them at work I just couldn't make it in anymore. I just didn't have any energy. I knew that they would be calling soon and telling me that I had to re-negotiate my time, but they had been so good, the hospital had never once complained about my schedule. I just appreciated everybody and would call and tell them how much I appreciated their flexibility.

The next to the last chemo treatment was the one that really took most of my energy, and I just couldn't function any longer. I finally became so depressed I called Dr. Malcolm's office and told him I just couldn't go on anymore. I was due for another treatment and he said we would sit and talk on Friday. Late on Friday Glenn and I sat in his office, waiting to hear news of whether or not I would get the treatment. He came out in the waiting room, it was so late and no one else was there. His news was my blood counts were too low and I couldn't be treated.

My white count was only 1000 after three weeks, and I felt I was just going on my very last leg. He reached over, grabbed my hand, and he said he knew how very sick I was, and we would try again next week. We would also talk about the rest of the treatments as I still had three more to go.

On Tuesday of the next week I began to feel a little bit more human again. It was as if those few days before my treatment was due I could almost see that there was a light at the end of the deep tunnel that I found myself in, and I would begin to feel good again. I felt more depressed to think I had to go take more drugs, and feel sick again.

I decided emotionally it might be good to go in and try to work. I went in and had managed to pretty much put together the uniform study I had been working on, and I had to put a presentation together for the policy and procedure committee. I woke up that morning feeling almost human again. I had worked on a nice flip chart type of presentation and felt ready to give it to the committee. I remember my boss was there, and a lot of people on the committee that I knew. Everyone said I did a nice job, and I felt proud of the work that I had done. It was one of the few highlights that I had had at work for a long time.

It just seemed I was working with a cloud that was always hanging over my head. I didn't feel I could think very clearly, and wondered if I really responded to people in an appropriate way. So many were so supportive and so good, but it seemed like they had lost their eye contact with me. It seemed to me, anyway, that people often would look away, or they'd say things like, "you look good."

My face was so round, I couldn't believe they would say I looked good. But I continued and would thank them, and then go on. Things seemed superficial. People didn't seem to know what to say to me, and the feeling was reciprocal, I didn't have much to say to them. Small talk sort of took over, and I spent a lot of time in my office working on paperwork. I did have a new office mate and Elaine and I continued to get to know each other better and better. That was a highlight for me.

I wondered what I would be like when I got through these treatments, if I would have any brain cells left. It just seemed such a struggle to even think. How I dreaded going for those next treatments. Friday came and I knew I had to go in there. I knew I had to do it and was so depressed. Dr. Malcolm had said we would talk, and I hoped beyond my wildest dreams that maybe this might be my last treatment. It was treatment number six. He'd said six months and I had almost done six months of treatment, but I knew that he really wanted me to have eight as everyone had said eight treatments would be the magic number for me.

I remember that day well as it was so beautiful. Where that sun came from I'm not sure, but it was beautiful. I'd worked part of the day and left early. Glenn and I drove to Dr. Malcolm's office. I went back to what I call my green room, with the green leather chair, and sat there. Susan gave me the Atavan under my tongue and the Zofran, and Dr., Malcolm came in. Susan had started the treatment and he sat there and looked at my chart.

He said this would be my last treatment and I couldn't believe it! It was all I could do to hold back the tears. He continued, he didn't think it would do any more good, the counts had been so low, and it just wasn't going to do anymore good. We had done almost six months and the tumor was small. This was all we were going to do. Those were the most beautiful words, and I couldn't believe it.

The treatment was the same as it had always been - the smash in the nose, the nausea. We had tried holding ice in my mouth to try to decrease the sores, but it didn't really work. So this time we didn't do it. It seemed to make me gag more when holding the ice in there. I just sat there while Susan pushed the drugs in, thinking for the vary last time I'd have to be doing this. Yet, in the back of my mind I wondered it was going to be enough. Would this be enough to have done the trick? Will it have killed all those awful cancer cells that had been floating around in my body? I felt that it was the right decision.

I remember I got home and called my Mom and called Glenn's Mom. I called all of our friends and told them I had my last treatment and I didn't have to finish. I didn't have to do anymore! It was truly a red letter day on my calendar, one that I will never, ever forget.

CHAPTER SIXTEEN

The Adoption

I wish I could say that the last treatment went very well, but I was just as sick with it as I had been with the previous treatments. I still had terrible problems with my bowel. Constipation had become such a source of pain, it was ruling my life. I would wake up in the morning and wonder when was the last time I went to the bathroom? Did I need cronulac today? How many pericolace do I take, ten or twelve?" It was such a difficult time, trying to manage my weight and my bowels, and yet trying to be positive because I had completed my treatments. My mind got bogged down and caught up in that film of the very last treatment. I got just as sick with this last as I had been with all of the ones before. I just took my Atavan and slept.

The people at the hospital called and asked me if I could re-negotiate my sick time. They wanted me to really try to come back the first of February, but I didn't know if I could handle it or not. I decided that I would go ahead and give it a try. I wanted to see if I could go back and work my full 72-hour pay period. I told them I would start the first week in February, full-time. I knew that it would have been two weeks after my last treatment, and I should be feeling a bit better, at least emotionally.

My first day back to work was, thankfully, uneventful. I tried to make rounds on all the units, and let people know that I had received my last treatment. People seemed genuinely happy for me. But, I still felt that they couldn't look me straight in the eye. They often looked away, or they would glance and then look down at the floor. I had trouble finding clothes to wear. I didn't have that many that had elastic, or were big enough. My mom got me a very pretty green skirt and sweater for Christmas. I managed to put a rubber band and expand it about five inches at the waist and pull the sweater over it. It had pressed down pleats, so I could just roll it and make it shorter, and wear it. I wore that every other day to work, alternating it with an old denim skirt with elastic that I could stretch and put around me. Then I wore a vest type sweater over it so people couldn't see that I could not button it clear to the top. I learned all kinds of fancy techniques in which I could wear some of my clothes, by using either big safety pins or rubber bands or rolling them up high enough so that I could manage to get them over my hips.

Dr. Malcolm and my family believed that it was too early for me to try to diet, but could just try to watch what I would eat. That had always worked in the past, so I had begun watching and trying to eat in a much more healthful way. I was depressed. The one thing that had plagued me on the Decadron was a pure, utter, and complete craving for chocolate. I've never been a "Chocaholic," and never really craved chocolate like a lot of people. But that last month it was one of the few things I wanted to eat. I would go to sleep thinking about Hershey Kisses! I would sit down and eat a pound of Hershey Kisses in a ten minute time period. The worst part was I didn't even care.

Another sign of the severe depression that I found myself in was that I kept working and pushing hard. I managed to make it to my birthday on the 7th. I knew that I had to get my driver's license. I stopped at the Bureau on the way home. I panicked at the thought that I would have to have my picture taken, my fat little round face and wig on my Driver's License for the next three years! I just swallowed my pride and stood up there and made funny comments about my chipmunk cheeks to the girl who was taking my picture. She told me that her mother had gone through the same thing a couple of years before. She had put on sixty pounds but never lost it. I thought that's not what I needed to hear! Someone else had put on more weight than I had, and they never lost it. I began to feel panicky inside, wondering if I would ever loose the weight. But I kept pushing and kept on going. During cold weather I would wear coats and try to disguise the extra pounds. I wore a lab coat at work which hid a lot of the layers of fat.

I still had moments of intense sadness when I would look at my body. I called the new breast an 'it' or a 'he.' I felt it was not me, or that it belonged to Dr. Kurtzman. One day Glenn suggested I should adopt 'it.' After all, it was me but, just looked as if I had surgery on the breast. I accused him of being crazy and dismissed the idea entirely.

A few days later Glenn's words came back to me Adopt 'it.' I stood naked from the waist up and looked in the mirror. "Before I had boobies, now I have only one boobie. I should adopt it, after all I do have my life. So, I named it Boobette. That night when Glenn came home, I introduced him to Boobette.

I was surprised that weekend when Vere and Diane stopped by with birthday presents for me. I couldn't believe it. I had been sleeping on the sofa, when they stopped by. They brought a beautiful costume jewelry pin, with some towels and pot holders that matched my dishes. We had a very nice visit with them and I felt better about the family. It was the first visit I'd had in months and it felt good. Shawn even came bringing me a birthday gift, and I got a few birthday cards. It wasn't so much that it was my birthday, it was the thought that someone remembered. My Mom did her usual and gave me $20. She always does the same for all of us. It was a good weekend. I rested a lot, did my Sunday School class and managed to get up Monday morning to go to work.

That week would be the test. Could I truly make it through? I pushed hard. We had written a proposal to do a research project at the hospital through the American Association of Critical Care Nurses, and I was to be the coordinator for the program. I had to present the proposal to the physicians at their meeting. Of course, I wore the blue dress I had been wearing all along with the elastic in the back, and my lab coat. I managed to get their permission to do the research. We had to have thirty patients by the end of March to be entered into the study.

This was another project that I felt good about. I had managed to write proposals and, along with the help of some fantastic nurses in our hospital, had managed to get our hospital involved in this national research project. We were the only other hospital to be involved and I felt a real urgency to make sure we were able to enroll our thirty patients in the time that we had left.

It became my main focus during February to talk with the right people and have the patients enrolled. It was actually a lot of fun to go in and talk with them. Some of them would ask me if I'd ever had to make big life-changing decisions. I told them that I was a "recovering cancer patient." I don't know when I started using that term, but it just came to me at some point. Somewhere I started using it and it gave me a very positive attitude. I felt the depression that had long enveloped my mind begin to leave.

I had hoped that some of the symptoms that I had from the chemotherapy would begin to dissipate by March but they didn't. I continued to have the conjunctivitis, the mouth sores, and the severe constipation. The burning in my GI tract had never really left from the very first chemo treatment and I couldn't eat anything that was spicy or take one sip of any kind of juice or pop. The only thing that I could drink was water, tea or coffee. Even coffee, my wonderful coffee, didn't taste right so I didn't drink very much of it. I became more guarded about what I put into my stomach, and continued on the Tagamet.

I had not had any menstrual periods on the chemotherapy. They had totally stopped. Around the holidays I started having hot flashes that continued even after I started back to work, although they weren't too terribly bad. In March, I did manage to have my first period. It was just like I had always had, even starting on the same day I'd started for years. I thought that this might help me start loosing weight. Dr. Malcolm wasn't very thrilled that I had started my period, and he actually looked kind of worried. But I was happy. I thought that this would be the key to loosing the extra weight.

March was a big month at work. I was putting patients on the study and getting other projects together. Administration had decided to combine some of our critical care units and change the nursing staffing. This meant that there were going to be some major educational interventions that would have to be done. I was involved in that and it scared me. Could I do it? They told me that I would be the one to be setting up the educational programs. I felt overwhelmed and wondered how in the world I would get all that work done. I felt as if I wanted to run away and not even be a nurse anymore. I felt such a tremendous burden.

In order to cope with this overwhelming feeling I decided to sit down with my manager and come up with a plan. It didn't seem so difficult once I had it in place. Once the plan was approved, we brought a group of people together who were willing to volunteer their services to help with some of the education. This way, it would not all fall on my shoulders. The first course was a pharmacology course that I had put together the year before. With some improvements in the curriculum, we were able to begin the program the first of April.

I was busy at work and it was good to be that busy. I began to feel that some of my thinking ability was becoming a little sharper, a little more clear. I had even managed to loose three whole pounds! I could not believe I was down to 153. With this encouragement, I decided to go ahead and start a real good weight-loss program. I decided on one that was high in protein and vitamins. I went to Dr. Malcolm and explained the program to him. He agreed that as long as I chose not to lose more than one pound a week he would let me give it a try. He insisted that I would need to have my blood counts checked and he would keep very close tabs on me.

I started the weight loss program and began to feel better just from the rejuvenation of thinking that maybe I could finally get some of those ugly pounds off. I became determined to have the weight half gone by the end of May. My grandparents were going to be married seventy years and we had planned a big family reunion to celebrate. I wanted it to be all gone, but I knew that would be unrealistic. Maybe I could have half of it gone.

The weight loss became my main focus. Along with the focus on education at work and coordination of multiple meetings and some helping with policies and procedures, I managed to fill my time. My manager had taken away my chair position of the Critical Care Policies and Procedures Committee that year. I felt sad and had some self doubts that maybe I had let them down and had not done a good job and I felt guilty. Some thoughts like this would come to mind and I would go to my office and see memos that I had written but did not remember writing. I knew it was me - it was my signature. Had being on chemotherapy affected me so dramatically? I wondered how I did act and respond all those weeks and months.

We managed to enroll all of our thirty patients for the research study. We had a two week reprieve and that gave us the time we needed to have everything ready by the 31st of March. I felt a very real sense of accomplishment. Our hospital was recognized and everybody seemed to be pleased that we were involved in this important research project.

I started to develop the other educational programs that were going to be needed. It was nice to have people send their names as volunteers. I had known some of those who volunteered since my very first day at the hospital, and here they were supporting me again. It felt good.

The changes that were going on within the critical care area were frustrating. People were upset by the changes and I knew from a professional perspective, the nurses in general did not feel valued. But yet, I did see our administration make a genuine effort to try to improve and make sure each and every one had positions. I knew from my experience in the other hospital when I was a patient that some of the nurses did not feel valued; they felt short changed. They did not always have the time to take care of their patients the way they wanted to and sadly, I also knew realistically that some of them wouldn't have taken good care of their patients even if they did not have heavy schedules. I do not know what the ingredient is that makes some nurses want to do a good job no matter what, while others just do not have the desire at all. I had a real feeling for our nurses, and a real anger and sense of frustration as I remembered the kind of care that I had received when I was sick.

My body continued to fight severe fatigue. I really had believed everyone when they told me that my energy level would return very soon after completing the chemotherapy. However, it did not return as readily as I had hoped or as I had expected it would. The only thing that I had noticed was that my brain began to function a little more clearly. The mouth sores did not last as long or come quite as frequently. But, the conjunctivitis and the constipation still plagued my body well into the middle of May.

By the end of May, when the reunion rolled around, I had only lost ten pounds. I tried to tell myself to be thankful that I had been able to loose that. but still could not get into any of my dresses, except the old blue one with the elastic in the back. I wore it anyway! I did have the courage to take my wig off when my hair was still relatively sparse. My hairdresser cut it and I had a perm. It seemed as if there were some kind of fertilizer being used as my hair was coming in very thick. It actually looked better than it did before. Although it was very short, at least I could go to the reunion with my own hair!

I wore the old blue dress and saw my Grandparents, cousins, aunts and uncles. It was a good day, we had a good time and actually, it was a very nice weekend. We had time to do wonderful family things like sitting and talking and renewing family ties. My family was glad to see me looking so well. I could not see it in myself, but it really didn't matter, I was just glad to be there and was truly beginning to feel glad to be alive.

I had seen my friend at work who was going through chemotherapy. I saw her struggling, as I knew I had struggled. I continued to try to keep in touch with her and send her notes to let her know that we continued to pray for her in my Sunday School class. I saw too that the Decadron was doing a number on her body. I understood the frustration that she was beginning to feel. When we talked, it was about chemotherapy and we laughed about it being like having the flu when you're at work, or of not being able to go home and lay down. When you are at home lying down and your mind sometimes plays tricks on you and tells you that you would feel better if you lay down. The trouble is that you realize that you **are** lying down.

One thing that I tried to do was to keep my sense of humor. I continued the comments about my feet looking up at the rest of my body asking what was happening up there. You're not losing that weight fast enough. You've got to keep going. We're dying down here.

My ankles continued to hurt and I had some hard nodes on the knuckle of my right hand that made my hand hurt with a deep, arthritic type of pain. Dr. Malcolm treated me for arthritis even though the tests came back negative. The node enlargement and the pain continued.

I missed my period in June but it didn't bother me too much. The hot flashes that I'd been having intensified, and the weight loss slowed down. I could not seem to loose even a half-pound. I was very strict with my diet and weighed in every day. I did everything that the counselors in the diet center asked me to do. I still had bad days when I would wake up with conjunctivitis or sores in my mouth and I still had bouts of depression.

I decided that it was time to try to think of ways to get out of the depression. One of the things I thought might make me feel better would be to go ahead and get the cosmetic piece done to 'Boobette." I made an appointment and went to see Dr. Kurtzman. We talked about my weight loss program and he agreed that I still needed to loose more weight. He did agree however, to go ahead and do the nipple reconstruction and liposuction for the extra fat that he had put into 'Boobette" under a local. I took a full day off for the visit and that did seem to help with some of the depression that I was still feeling.

I decided to try a different type of diet, a more strict kind of diet than the one I had been on. The diet counselors and I talked about trying to fool my body and jolt it into realizing that it needed to loose the weight. My ankles still hurt very badly and it was very difficult to walk around.

The weather was beginning to change and it was warmer now. I wanted to be able to wear some comfortable, cool clothes. I did not feel I could afford to go out and buy more "fat" clothes for the summertime.

By the time my surgery rolled around, I had lost almost twenty pounds and was beginning to feel better about myself. The surgery was done under local anesthesia and I remember talking all the way through the procedure. The nursing staff was wonderful and had come early that morning to introduce themselves. They were very supportive and I was very nervous about the procedure itself. Even though I knew that 'Boobette' did not have any feeling, I still had fear of pain. The nurses and I talked a lot about my phantom pain. I had continued to feel that at times I had my old nipple and my old breast back. I even, at times, still had difficulties with the old electric pain in my arm, but it had gotten better, and I was able to tolerate it.

Glenn went with me the day of the procedure. We were both in a very jovial mood. He had taken a vacation day and it was my day off. It was sort of a renewal time for us. He seemed happier than he had been in a long time. That made me feel happy. The procedure lasted quite a while. Dr. Kurtzman took a little piece of tissue from inside of my thigh and reconstructed a nipple. He explained everything as he did it. A young resident helped him with the surgery. I could hear them talking but they would not let me watch any of the procedure. I was curious and wanted to see what was going on, while at the same time I was a little nervous about watching.

The last part of the procedure was very, very difficult. This involved liposuction of the extra fat out of the reconstructed breast. It was excruciatingly painful and it seemed as if he was just scraping the ribs on my chest. There was a lot of pressure, a lot of pain, and I cried. The nurse never left my side, staying with me holding my hand, and telling me I was doing well. I don't know how you are supposed to act with that kind of pain. But I do know that the nurses presence and her reassurance made it bearable. She was fantastic, they all were. They kept talking to me, telling me that I looked good and that I had done well to loose as much weight as I did. Any conversation to keep my mind off of the pain.

They knew more about the Decadron weight than anyone else and told me how difficult it is to get the pounds off, and that it is much harder to get steroid weight off than weight gain from overeating. I teasingly said, the only thing I ate that I truly enjoyed the whole time I was on chemotherapy was chocolate, especially Hershey Kisses. We talked about how those Hershey Kisses had certainly 'kissed' my rump. But, the conversation made the procedure tolerable, except for the pain.

I could not wait to see my nipple. But I was in for a big disappointment as Dr. Kurtzman had used some kind of thick gauze. It stood up about an inch at the end of my breast. You could see where he made little sutures in it. It looked like a daisy stuck on the end of 'Boobette.' You could not see any of the tissue that he had grafted onto the site at all. Just this big daisy-like dressing. I wanted to see what it was going to look like, but he said no to that request. I would have to wait another week.

I kind of chuckled and thought about having to go around with a daisy on my boob for a whole week. Dr. Kurtzman said that this was all part of the procedure and that indeed I would have to wait a week. I felt good as Glenn and I got into the car. He asked if I had gotten to see the nipple and I told him no but that I had a Daisy on the end of my breast. We both laughed and I told him I would show him when we got home.

I felt fine after the surgery so Glenn and I decided to go window shopping. We both had the day off, I had no ill effects and, for the first time in a long while I felt like going shopping. My mother had always said that I could shop until I drop any day of the week. Cancer and the chemotherapy had certainly changed my attitude about a lot of things, even that. Shopping had become almost like a plague, it was something that I dreaded and hated. I no longer enjoyed it at all. But today was different. The sun was shining and it was a beautiful day.

We did a lot of looking that day. We didn't really buy very much. The one thing that we did buy was a very inexpensive watch. I had never bought myself a watch before but I found a pretty one with a blue edge and bought it. Glenn and I decided that it was a new time in our lives and that I should start it with a new watch. The rest of the day was happy. We ate out, I had my diet food, and we drove home talking and laughing, feeling better than we had for a very long time.

I went to work on Monday with a new spirit. I managed to work extra that week so I was able to take the afternoon off to go back to Dr. Kurtzman. I couldn't wait to see what he had done to 'Boobette.' When we arrived Debbie greeted us with her usual upbeat welcome. Debbie was the one who removed the daisy dressing. and I was totally amazed. The first thing that Debbie said to me was not to be surprised by the size, it would shrink to a more normal size. I was not surprised by the size, it looked fine to me. I was surprised at how real it looked. In fact, it looked absolutely fantastic! It was wonderful! I felt like my life was coming back together. You could really tell that the liposuction had worked. Both breasts were very much the same size.

There was one problem. 'Boobette' was coming up on her first birthday, but the other was over thirty years old and you could tell. She drooped, did not look like she had any energy. 'Boobette' looked perky. I told Dr. Kurtzman my concerns and wanted 'Boobie' to be uplifted, whatever he had to do, whatever that was called, a mastoplexy. All that I could think to say was, just do it.

As I was beginning to loose weight, I noticed that on the right side where the tissue had been removed from my original surgery had become weaker. I felt pulling when I did any kind of exercise or any kind of movement. The doctor told me that he did not think it was a hernia, but rather a weak place in the abdomen. To me it looked like a hernia and it felt uncomfortable on the inside. It concerned me enough to question him about the extent of the surgical procedure to repair it if indeed it were a hernia. He explained that it was not major surgery. He could go in and strengthen the wall with a few extra sutures. I would probably miss only two or three weeks at work. He did recommend loosing a few more pounds before having the procedure.

Dr. Kurtzman outlined the additional procedures that I would need to complete the process. In addition to the hernia repair, he recommended that I have the mastoplexy at the same time. I would also have my new nipple "tattoo" so it would be the same color as the other. He explained that both procedures could be done at the same time. He wanted to wait about two months to assure the added weight loss.

To help the time pass more quickly, I continued my diet and worked hard putting programs together for the nurses. I tried to empathize with them as they were going through the trials of combining units. My manager had taken a maternity leave and decided not to return to work. I was very sad, almost to the point of grief that she had decided not to return. We had such a good relationship and I really missed her.

Yet it was also a frustrating time both at work and with my diet. I continued to struggle with the pounds and I was tired of the high protein foods. I was feeling tired and needed a bit of a vacation. I had saved all of my sick and vacation time for the surgery and had none available for a vacation. I would have to be careful with any time that I might be able to take off, even just a few days.

In August, Glenn and I decided to take a four-day weekend and just get away. Someplace, anyplace. We did not really know where we were going to go. We decided to go to Gatlinburg as we had never been there, it would be a new adventure. We got up early Saturday morning and just started to drive. It was such an ugly day, raining, and cold for August and overall gloomy. We surprised ourselves by making it all the way to Gatlinburg. We spent three wonderful days shopping in the outlet stores. We went to a place called the Dixie Stampede and stamped our feet and laughed and giggled. We had the best three days of shopping and fun and being together that we had had in a very long time. It was wonderful!

When we got back, I called Dr. Kurtzman's office to set up an appointment for the "final" surgical procedures. After all, I had lost thirty pounds and was ready to get on with my life. I was counting on being ready for skiing in the winter and needed to get back to exercises to get my legs ready for the slopes. We set up the surgery for August 31, just a little over one year from my original surgery.

The night before the surgery Glenn seemed a little concerned and told me that I did not need the surgery just because my right side "stuck out" a little bit. He didn't think it looked that bad. I was touched by his concern but tried to explain that I was not doing it for cosmetic reasons. I was doing it because of the pulling sensations. I had been working on the units doing some actual bedside care again, and I found that I just couldn't lift or pull on a patient in any way without a tremendous feeling of a bulging sensation in my right side.

The next morning I got up at 4:00 a.m. to get ready for the drive. But this time was different and I wasn't depressed. I actually felt excited and glad this would be the end!

The surgery went well except that it lasted a little longer than expected. The hernia was larger than expected and required quite a bit of repair. When Dr. Kurtzman pulled the muscle to the right, the navel that he had reconstructed for me the year before also pulled over. At that point he had to go in and reopen the left side as well. So, I ended up with an incision, once again, from hip bone to hip bone.

I woke up in my room thinking how bad it hurt and once again I felt like I had my chin sewed to my knees. I couldn't straighten back up. Deja Vu! But this time it was different, a lot easier. Memories did come back that weren't always the most pleasant ones. But God, in all of His glory, had once again taken care of it for me.

In the bed next to me was another woman, a patient of Dr. Kurtzman, who had gone through the same surgery a year before. She, too, had pulled out some stitches and had to have them redone. Her name was Bonnie and we shared a lot of conversation. We talked all through the evening until about 2 a.m. We woke up at 6 a.m. and started talking again, and became instant friends. It was an immediate liking and bonding with each other. When Dr. Kurtzman came in on rounds to release us, we sat on the edge of our beds and made jokes and teased him. We all laughed about what a mistake it was for him to put both of us in the same room. We told him that we compared his stitches and his work. He was wonderful, laughing and joking along with us.

I asked him to draw me a picture so I understood a little bit more of what he had done. He also gave me my instructions to take it easy and not to think about going back to work in three weeks. I had to go home with the wonderful Jackson-Pratt tube in my abdomen. I remembered a year ago and how frightened I had been of that. How I really didn't want to go home with the tube, but this year I had the confidence that I could handle it. The tube would be removed on Thursday, which wasn't such a long time. But then he threw me a curve. saying, "Well you're a nurse, just take the sutures out and pull the tube out."

I looked at him with surprise and said, "I don't know if I can do that or not, but I'll try. I will call you Thursday morning if I can't do it." As I thought about it, I remembered that my sister is a nurse, she can come and pull it out. So I just made up my mind that I would ask Shawn to come and do this for me.

I went home pretty tired and groggy. I took it pretty easy the rest of the week waiting for Thursday to come. The drainage had diminished and the tube was ready to be removed on time. Shawn came over and together we removed the tube. I could tell she thought it was a pretty good size by the way her pupils dilated. I laughed at her because to me it looked a lot smaller then it had the year before.

Slowly my strength came back. I can look back on a lot of things over the past year. I think of the good things that have happened, and I remember the bad. The things that I remember most about the bad days are the times that I was the loneliest and the most depressed. Those days were when I thought I would never get well, that the chemo would never end, and I would never be able to get back into my old clothes. I now can get back into all of my old clothes, and, I look pretty much like Sue again.

Life is good again, maybe even better because I enjoy it more. Glenn is still working hard and back to traveling. Melissa is in school and doing well. She smiles more now. I'm working full-time, back at the bedside on a part-time basis and love it all. I still teach Sunday School class and they continue to be a support for me. I'm learning and learning.....to praise the Lord everyday.

I have learned a lot. I have learned to be thankful for the way I am now. I don't feel I'm overweight, although for years I always felt like I was a very heavy short woman. I realize now that was a misconception in my head. So many things have changed for me and I have a different confidence. I have a different level of understanding and I feel that I can be a better nurse. I know that I am a better wife and mother, and for that I just praise the Lord.

CHAPTER SEVENTEEN

Reconstruction

The following pages contain pictures of women who have had various types of reconstruction. This chapter has been included because I feel strongly that it is important to actually see some of the choices that women have and to see the normal appearance that can be obtained through plastic surgery. I want you to see the symmetry and the balance that can be possible through reconstruction. When faced with the need to make the choice, there may be times when you will think of the new breast as only a mound of tissue. However, understanding the choices you have and the types of procedures available, you will be more comfortable in knowing you **CAN** have very normal appearing breasts. The pictures in this chapter are of real life women, they are not models nor are they diagrams.

Dr. Kurtzman, Debbie, and Bonnie continue to be a very important support to me and to my family. I appreciate them daily. I recently spoke with one of Dr. Kurtzman's patients who was about to have the same surgical procedure that I had undergone. During our conversation she commented that her concern about her appearance after the surgery might make people think she was being vain. My response to her was total reassurance that she was just being a woman, and there is nothing wrong with that!

The diagnosis of cancer, the actual breast surgery, chemotherapy, and reconstruction can cause a very deep emotional trauma for the majority of women. They need the support of their physician, the nurses and every member of the health care team.

Everyone will need health care at some time during their lifetime, and we all need a · big dose of TLC now and then!

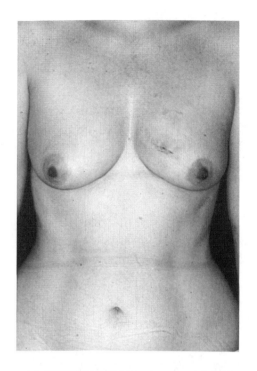

PATIENT ONE

A 40 year old woman with biopsy proven left breast carcinoma. She underwent a left mastectomy with immediate reconstruction. A free TRAM (trans rectus abdominis myocutaneous) flap was utilized for the reconstruction. The abdominal tissue is the same tissue as in the pedicled TRAM, it is totally detached from the body and its viability maintained by attaching it to an artery and vein to the axilla. Subsequently, she unerwent nipple reconstruction and a mastoplexy (lift) of the right breast to improve symmetry.

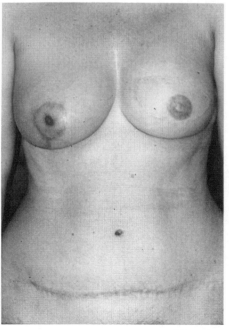

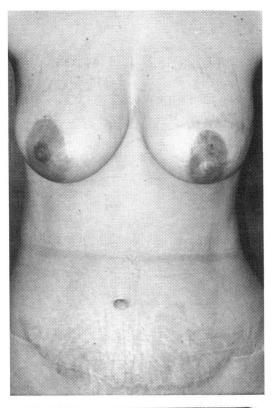

PATIENT TWO

A 38 year old mother of three who required a left mastectomy for cancer. Utilizing the excess abdominal tissue, she underwent a pedicled TRAM flap which remains attached to the rectus absominis muscles and transferred to the chest. The large amount of tissue utilized for this flap is outlined on the abdominal wall. Once transferred, an abdominoplasty (tummy-tuck) closure reconstructs the abdominal wall. Subsequently she underwent nipple reconstruction and tattooing. From the side view, the tightening of the abdomen is noted. Symmetric amount of ptosis (droopiness) is created by the reconstruction.

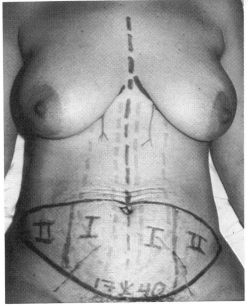

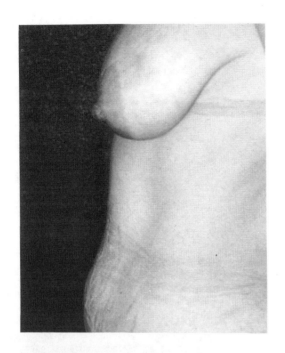

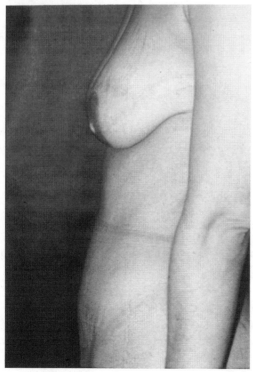

133

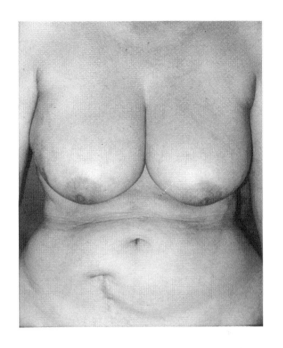

PATIENT THREE

A 46 year old woman with a cancer of the right breast tissue. The abdonimal tissue (TRAM flap) was used to reconstruct the right breast. The overlying skin is removed and the tissue buried underneath the chest skin to provide the breast mound. She subsequently underwent revision of the right breast with nipple reconstruction and tattooing. At the same time, she underwent a breast reduction on the left to decrease the size of the breast and provide symmetry. Approximately one pound of tissue was removed from the left breast.

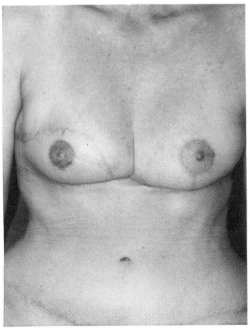

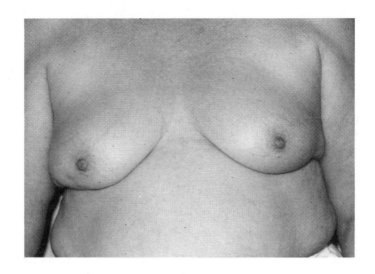

PATIENT FOUR

A 65 year old woman with a cancer of the right breast. She underwent
a right mastectomy and immediate placement of a tissue expander
(subcutaneous balloon). With tissue expansion, it is necessary to initially
overinflate the chest skin for subsequent placement of the permanent implant.
This improves the shape of the breast and aides in maintaining its softness.
Four months after full expansion is achieved, an exchange for a permanent
implant is made. At the same time, a mastopexy (breast lift) on the
left provides symmetry. Subsequently she underwent nipple reconsturction
on the right.

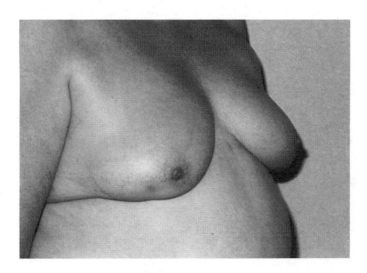

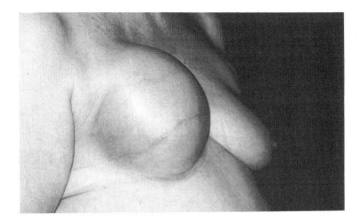

Over Expansion

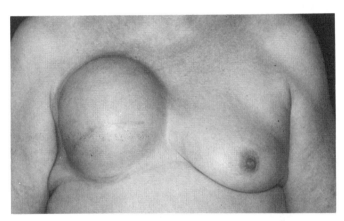

Post Extender Exchange

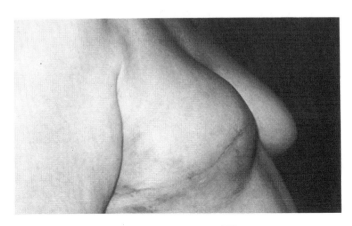

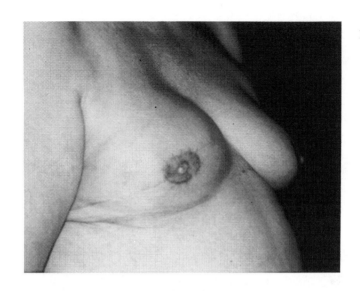

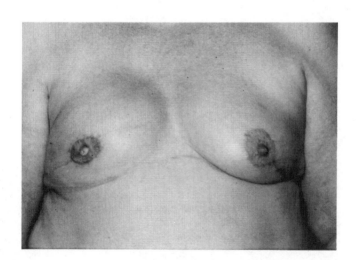

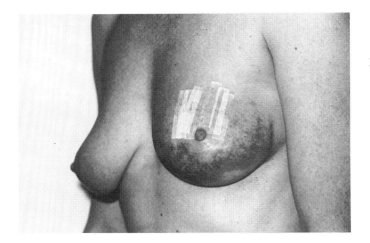

PATIENT FIVE

A 42 year old woman with bilateral breast cancer. She underwent a bilateral mastectomy and placement of tissue expanders. Depicted is the overexpansion necessary to maintain a soft breast. Once the expanders are exchanged for permanebt implants, the shape, contour, and size of the breast is significantly improved. Subsequently, she underwent nipple reconstruction and areolar tattooing to complete the reconstruction.

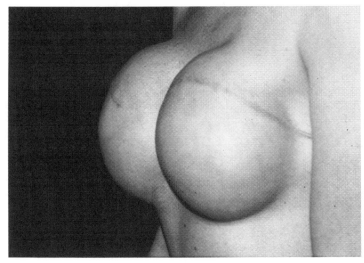

Over Expansion

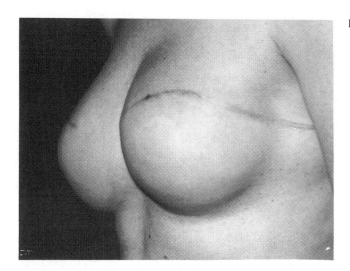

Post Expander Exchange

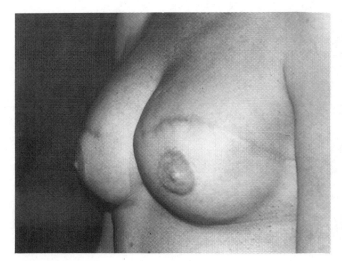

Post Nipple-Areolar

139

CHAPTER EIGHTEEN

When The Tulips Bloom

I can hardly believe I've been off chemotherapy for over a year now. My tulips are blooming brightly in the yard. They look so beautiful, more beautiful than ever before. I wake up every morning praising my Lord for all the wonderful things He has done for me. I still have bouts of sadness but they are short-lived. My heart now aches for others who are experiencing painful situations because now I truly understand. It is as though I have this kinship for others who are experiencing pain. I don't understand if these difficulties are due to an increase in disease or, if it 's age-related; I suspect it's both. I do know the only way to get through it is to pray and trust the Lord to pull you through somehow. I've also shared with you my story in hopes it will help someone else. It has been difficult for me to tell you some of my most intimate thoughts, putting them on paper for the whole world to read. But, my message is clear and simple.

Michele Carson in her article, "Anxiety in the ICU," said it best: "Illness alters an individual's physical integrity, state of well-being, and ability to be independent." it doesn't matter whether you are a health care professional or a family member, you need to remember this. When you become ill, you loose control of YOUR life. We need kind, understanding people around us and ones with BIG listening and hearing ears. I often tell my nurses about intuitive nursing. Intuitive nursing is being so in touch with that patient that you can tell what is going on even before the physical symptoms appear. We also need more intuitive relationships. People who care so much that they can perceive feelings before real problems develop. This can, and is, done by constantly affirming and valuing people where they are.

I've been editing this book for the last time and I can now see that it has truly been written in stages over the last three years. Times of complete utter sadness, despair, confusion and anger have each had priority in my life. I still deal with the anger when I think back to the care I received, but now I use it to focus on others and where they are in their lives. I know we all have periods in our lives during which we wish we could do some things differently, but we know we can't. I believe that if people in health care can see how important their roles are along with the interactions they have with the patients, maybe, just maybe, they will look inside and change the things that need to be changed. I know that my and Glenn's illnesses have changed me and how I interact with my patients and with people in general. I value them more than I ever did.

Let me share an example of what I am talking about. Recently I took care of an 82 year old woman who was returning from having a mastectomy. One of the first things she said to me as she was beginning to wake up from the anesthetic was, "What do I put in my bra now?" No one had spoken with this woman about anything other than her current need for surgery. The surgeon thought because she was 82, loosing a breast would not mean anything to her. He was wrong. This woman still worked three days a week and was concerned about her clothes and her appearance. I talked with her about prostheses and bras, and support groups and I gave her my home phone number to call me when she got home.

I firmly believe in the value of a second opinion and I want to tell you that you will NOT offend anyone. Most doctors feel more comfortable with the decisions that are made after second opinions. After all, it is your body and you are the one who has to live with it.

Physically I am doing well. My strength is back to my normal. I still don't like to exercise but I force myself to do it. Boobette looks great. She has little tiny white lines not scares and she looks remarkably like Boobie. I take her everywhere I go. My arm still has those electric type pains and is numb from my elbow up including most of my shoulder. I've learned to live with this and I feel this is a very small price to pay. However, I thought you might like to know how I am now. My weight is normal and I can fit in most of my clothes. I am very happy I made the decision I did and have no regrets. I still do breast self exams every month and I now know Boobette as well as I know Boobie. So, there is still a message there for you; male or female, get to know your body then you will be able to tell your physician when it feels different to you.

Glenn is also doing well. His last CAT scan did not show anything but scar tissue where he had his surgery. He's still on Dilantin and still has muscle tremors "jerks" at night. Sometimes when he's very tired his speech will become slurred. However, he feels good and has no limitations that we've noted. Melissa is now a young woman and in many ways still dealing with these illnesses of her parents. She is doing well and should graduate next Spring, when the tulips bloom.

I hope on these few pages you have seen what God can do. It is my prayer that you will gain the courage to take control of your life. Don't let other people, regardless of title, physician, or not, try to discourage you. You must not be afraid to ask questions and to demand what is yours. I've had so many women say to me, "Sue, my doctor didn't give me a choice. He made the decision for me." That makes me incredibly sad!

An acquaintance was recently diagnosed with breast cancer. She called me in the depths of her dispair to hear what I had done. She was frightened and her physician had not discussed any options for her, only mastectomy right away. She came to my home, a perfect stranger, and we spoke for hours about her options. She did not choose the same kind of surgery I had, nor did I expect her to. But, I wanted her to know her options. She is now finished with her chemotherapy and is looking for a bright future with her family. I wrote this book to let other people know that they have choices concerning health care. You have the right to a second opinion. Karen and I were strangers but now I can pick up the phone, call her, and know we are like sisters. We have a bond that nothing can ever change. We went to the depths of despair, but God allowed us to return.

Karen is now going out and giving talks about her experience. I would like to share with you the original poem that Karen reads to begin each talk.

DARK TO DAWN
by

Karen Edds

One day all is bright and sunny
Your life is good and jokes are funny
Then you find an ominous lump
Your heart is pounding and you feel each thump.

Your Mammogram shows some calcification
And you sit in silence for an explanation
It's not good, probably cancer
We'll do a biopsy for the final answer.

You have the results...it was as you expected
Your mind races, how do you accept it?
You pray, Oh Heavenly Father keep me calm
As you lie awake waiting for the dawn.

God sent me many special people along the way
He gave me Susan Miller the very first day
She had finished what I was facing
That night she prayed for the Lord to embrace me
To lift me up and to hold me close
In those dark lonely days when I needed Him most.

It's hard sometimes to pray for yourself
In times when you're so consumed with what life has dealt
A friend will call with you on their mind
And say they are praying at that very time.

They share that during times like these
It's those who love you that are on their knee
Interceding on my behalf
It seems this difficult time will never pass.

Oh, I look good, there's a smile on my face
But the tears are falling...I can't keep pace
My husband holds me when words are absent
I thank God for his love and ever presence.

The surgery is finished...treatments are over
God has blessed me so that I must tell others
Sometimes it is as dark as it seems
But Jesus is there to give us back our dreams
Look to Him and you will find
You can make it through one day at a time.

To the ones that were always there
Thank you my friends for your special care
The cards, flowers, food and such
Trips to the doctor...taking me to lunch
I thank you all so very much.

Yes we can get through the crises in our lives. However as a nurse, I've learned a tremendous amount from these experiences and Karen said it very well.

What a fantastic lady you are, Karen. Thank you!

The lose of control that comes with illness takes its toll on the entire family. Sadness over what has changed and anxiety over the future still haunts you in the wee hours of the morning, but you find you have a new weapon to fight it and that is a courage to face whatever the future holds. Fear is always out there, but I will not let it run my life or that of my family.

The hope that this book will help others has been my goal. It has been difficult for me to finish because there are still so many feelings to share and things to tell you. I want people to read this book and see the feelings that we all experience when illness strikes, both from the perspective of the family and the patient. I want women and men, nurses and physicians, administrators and other health care providers, the President and his wife, to read this book and have a better understanding of what we go through when illness comes.

I know that I have been showered with love and affection beyond my wildest dreams. I know the Lord has allowed me to walk the Valley of the Shadow of Death to make me stronger and to give me the courage to write this book.

I call this book my love trilogy. I hope you see the love of the Lord on these pages and how each day is truly a gift from Him.

I hope you can see a real life love story between a man and a woman. I hope you can see a successful marriage that has survived. A love story that continues to get better and better.

I hope you can see my love for my nursing profession and how, if given the choice again, I would still become a nurse. I was recently asked to write what I would hope others would say about me and this is what I hope they would say: I loved Sue, not because she was a leader, not because she was a follower, but because she was someone nice to walk beside who journeyed with the Lord.

MY PRAYER

Thank you, Lord, for how far I have come. Thank you for my wonderful husband who is here with me today. Thank you for my daughter and our loving relationship, for my Mom and her love and support. Thank you for all my family and the love that we share.

Thank you, Lord, for my career and a place to work where I can help others who need my services everyday. Thank you, too, for friends and co-workers who make my work and life enjoyable.

Lord, I thank you for my church and all the people, where I can go to worship and praise You for the things You do for me and for others. And. Lord, last, but not least, I thank you for Carolyn Zagury who believes in You and me and our book.

Lord, now I ask You to hold in Your loving arms all those who are suffering physical and/or sometimes emotional pain. Give them the strength and the courage they need to find VICTORY in You. Amen!